Survival
Under Adversity

Robert E. Williams, MD, PhD, MPH, BTh

TEACH Services, Inc.
P U B L I S H I N G
www.TEACHServices.com • (800) 367-1844

World rights reserved. This book or any portion thereof may not be copied or reproduced in any form or manner whatever, except as provided by law, without the written permission of the publisher, except by a reviewer who may quote brief passages in a review.

The author assumes full responsibility for the accuracy of all facts and quotations as cited in this book. The opinions expressed in this book are the author's personal views and interpretations, and do not necessarily reflect those of the publisher.

This book is provided with the understanding that the publisher is not engaged in giving spiritual, legal, medical, or other professional advice. If authoritative advice is needed, the reader should seek the counsel of a competent professional.

Copyright © 2015 TEACH Services, Inc.
ISBN-13: 978-1-4796-0485-2 (Paperback)
ISBN-13: 978-1-4796-0486-9 (ePub)
ISBN-13: 978-1-4796-0487-6 (Mobi)
Library of Congress Control Number: 2015909709

All scriptures taken from the New King James Version®
Copyright © 1982 by Thomas Nelson. Used by permission. All rights reserved.

Cover image, "Against The Wind" by Liz Lemon Swindle,
used by permission www.LDSArt.com

This book is dedicated to my wife Gloria, who has stood by my side for over 60 years. Her faith in God and loving presence has been the source of encouragement that has helped me overcome adversity.

Introduction

From my elementary school days I encountered barriers in the form of negatives that challenged my achievements every step of the way. A renowned obeah man accosted me and predicted I would never make it through high school. Upon admission to college, I was pronounced stupid, illiterate, and primitive and was told it was useless to try to succeed academically.

A year after college my employer challenged me and said public opinion was against my ambition of becoming a physician, and I should give up the thought. When I was accepted to the University of Arkansas for premedical studies, that employer fired me and predicted I would never make it and that my ambition would lead me to disaster. My premed instructor said my result on his IQ test branded me a failure, and I would never make it.

When I was accepted to medical school, a physician said the survival rate in medical school was low and advised me to try being a nurse, not a doctor. In my second year of medical school, my bitter professor, out of revenge, threatened my entire career and gave me an F on my final exam. In my last semester of medical school, I was given fourteen days to pay off the balance on my school fees or forfeit my graduation. The negatives were like a nightmare trailing me every step of the way. I was continually facing the challenge of the obeah man who said I would never make it. I wondered if it was worth trying, if I was too ambitious, if I would add to the growing list of those who tried and failed or if I should continue striving to survive. I did strive and I did survive all of the adversities that came my way.

Today, with a background of international experiences I have earned a number of degrees: BTh (bachelor of theology), BS, MPH, PhD, and an MD. This book is dedicated to those who have a desire to achieve a goal, in particular those who are encountering adversities—adversities in the form of barriers that may be financial, cultural, genetic, social, religious, educational, or familial in nature. It is dedicated to those who are discouraged and are ready to give up because of the continual fear of failure. It is my hope and prayer that reading this book will stimulate, motivate, and educate you in your effort to survive these negative barriers to your success.

Table of Contents

Chapter 1-Surviving the Monster --- 7

Chapter 2-Surviving Vicious Complex ------------------------------ 11

Chapter 3-Surviving Public Opinion -------------------------------- 14

Chapter 4-Surviving Financial Pressure --------------------------- 18

Chapter 5-Why So Ambitious -- 22

Chapter 6-Surviving Counterfeits ----------------------------------- 27

Chapter 7-Surviving the Impossible -------------------------------- 30

Chapter 8-Surviving the Ultimate ----------------------------------- 33

Chapter 9-Surviving Trends -- 43

Chapter 10-You Are a Survivor ------------------------------------- 51

Chapter 11-Surviving Directions ----------------------------------- 63

Chapter 12-Surviving Phobias -------------------------------------- 77

Chapter 13-Surviving Love -- 81

Chapter 14-Facing Realities --- 89

Chapter 15-Yesterday -- 103

A Special Chapter-Surviving Some Health Issues ------------------ 106

Biographical Sketch -- 116

Chapter 1
Surviving the Monster
"You'll never make it"

In every man lies the possibility to succeed. The will to succeed exceeds the fear of failure. Christopher Columbus, on expressing his belief that the world was round, was considered a dreamer filled with fantasies. Kings and queens felt his attempt to prove his theory was unrealistic and did not merit the help he sought. In theory they said, "You will never make it."

The king and queen of Spain felt the potential benefits far exceeded the regrets in failing to do so, and they gave him three small ships: the Pinta, the Nina, and the Santa Maria. He encountered great difficulties and grave risks, but by the end of his third voyage, he had proven his theory to be a fact. He discovered a new world and opened the way for Vasco da Gama who founded the Cape of Good Hope and Ferdinand De Magellan who discovered the Strait of Magellan. To succeed in life, you need to believe in yourself, that you have what it takes to reach your goal.

> **To succeed in life, you need to believe in yourself, that you have what it takes to reach your goal.**

History is filled with men and women who were criticized. They met these struggles with self-confidence and survived their adversities. Here is a partial list of people who succeeded in life despite challenges:

- Charles Goodyear ventured and brought about the Goodyear tire in 1844.

- John Deere invented the steel plow in 1832 despite great difficulties.
- David McConnell founded Avon, the world-renowned women's shop that came about in 1886.
- Levi Straus produced Levi's jeans in 1873.
- Adolpus Busch introduced Budweiser beer in 1876.
- George Eastman invented the KODAK camera in 1888.
- Milton Hershey created HERSHEY'S milk chocolate bar in 1900.
- Willis Carrier invented modern air conditioning in 1902.
- David Sarnoff invented the radio in 1926.
- Ruth Handler gave us the Barbie doll in 1959.
- J. C. Nichols gave us the shopping mall in 1922.
- Sam Walton opened Walmart in 1962.
- Percy Spencer introduced the microwave oven in 1946.

The list grows longer each day, with men and women who, by sacrifice and amid mockery and criticism, have survived the negatives and helped to make the world an easier place to live.

The following timeline shows how one great man reached his career goals despite repeated setbacks. He lost his job in 1832. He failed in business in 1833. His sweetheart died in 1835. He had a nervous breakdown in 1836. He lost his bid for Congress in 1843. He was elected to Congress in 1846. He lost a nomination for Congress in 1848. He lost his bid for the U.S. Senate in 1854. He lost his nomination for vice president in 1856. He was defeated again for the Senate in 1858. Then he was elected president of the United States in 1860. These setbacks would have given most people an excuse to give up, but Abraham Lincoln was determined to reach his goal, and he survived many adversities. How strong is your determination to reach your goal?

One busy morning on my way to an appointment, I picked up a hitchhiker. After saying good morning, I asked him where I could take him, and he said, "Anywhere you are going." I was helping a hitchhiker without a goal, or vision. His destiny was anywhere?

This caused me to think of a verse from #232 in *The New Hymnal for American Youth*: "To every man there openeth a way, and ways and a way, the high soul climbs the high way and the low soul climbs the low. But in between on the misty flat the rest drifts to and fro. A man without a vision is a drifter."

As a young boy in elementary school, I inherited hatred from a famous obeah man because of a disagreement between my eldest brother and him.

An obeah man was considered a devil worshipper. He was feared by some because he was believed to have contact with evil spirits. Some believed he had the power to kill, condemn, and curse his enemies. Because of me he pronounced judgment on my school.

In those days after one finished elementary school you had the option of taking the first, second, and third local examinations as preliminary eligibility for secondary school. Each exam was taken after one year of intensive studies. Students from all the schools would meet at designated centers to take these exams on two consecutive Fridays. Ten of us were preparing for these exams at my school. The obeah man's judgment was that I would never make it and because of me nobody else would either. On hearing this all my peers decided to leave for another school four miles away. Since I was the target, I could not go with them. I was forced to decide whether I should continue or give up.

I remembered learning in Sabbath School that the Lord had promised that no weapon formed against one of His children would prosper and that those who trust in the Lord shall be like Mount Zion and shall mount up with eagle's wings. With those promises firmly in mind, my will to succeed far exceeded my fear of failure. I decided to keep going to school and not give up.

One morning on my way to class, I got into a conversation with another spiritualist who happened to have heard of my plight. A spiritualist was similar in character to an obeah man but not as dreaded. He complimented me on my determination to continue and promised he would give me a mound of yams if I succeeded. Thus, as the days went by, three things kept motivating me:

1. The faith I had that God would keep His promise. I had searched and discovered that He always had.
2. Those yams kept telling me, "You must make it. You can't afford to fail, we are yours." Every day as I passed by the garden, I reassured my claim on them.
3. I had convinced myself that I could and would make it.

The will to succeed grew stronger and stronger as the days went by, and I had no fear of failure. It was not in my vocabulary.

One year went by, and the day for my first exam came. To the amazement of everyone, I passed with exceptional scores. Unfortunately, all my friends who had succumbed to fear failed. Your greatest enemy is fear.

I managed to get the spiritualist to double his pledge of yams if I passed the second year. The next two years were easy sailing. I had accepted with gratitude the judgment of my enemy, and now I saw it as a challenge and a steppingstone. I passed my first, second, and third local exams with exceedingly high marks. I also enjoyed three mounds of yams provided from the spiritualist.

On the day when the results for the third local exams were posted, a friend who had taken the exam and seen the results ran to tell my mother that I had failed because he had not seen my name on the list. I inquired if he had passed. He had failed again. Therefore, I thought that since his name was not on the list, quite likely he would not have seen mine. Sure enough, my name was on the list.

There are certain persons who will tell you that you will never make it:
- Those who are failures themselves.
- Those who are pessimists who will always see failures.
- Those who see you as not being able to make it.
- You, when you become a captive of adversities.

Are you concerned about achieving your goal? Here is some proven advice.
- Do you believe in God? If you don't, you are not alone; there are many who don't. But if you do, then trust Him. He promised that if you ask, He will answer; if you seek, He will help you find; and if you knock, He will open. Those who believe in Him have proven these promises to be real.
- Do you believe that the Bible is God's Word? If you do, then read Psalm 1. Trust in the Lord at all times, and He will allow your hard work to shine through.
- Believe in yourself. Don't be turned around by the pessimist or by negative events or by obstacles.

"Success in life is a matter not so much of talent or opportunity as of concentration and perseverance."

C. W. Wendte said, "Success in life is a matter not so much of talent or opportunity as of concentration and perseverance." Go for it. You will make it.

Chapter 2
Surviving Vicious Complex
"Needless Try"

Sometimes we are tempted to think that a series of successes is an indicator that life is mapped out to be trouble-free and doors that were once closed will now be opened. We begin to live on experiences and become satisfied with only what our past achievements provide. As human beings we will never live long enough to exhaust the potentials of our mind. Intellectual growth should be progressive because if it is not challenged it will become dormant to the extent that we accept the negatives as the norm.

After three years of scholastic success, I struggled for almost three years to get a job. I applied to the superintendent of schools for a position as a teacher, but he told me that since I trusted so much in God I should trust Him for a job.

There were days I survived on small bits of sugar cane because I had no money to buy bread. I finally resorted to rearing goats and farming. I did menial tasks to help my mother meet the demands for the daily basics.

After three years I applied and was accepted to college. My scholastic status qualified me for form IV, which meant five years of study. I pleaded with the dean of the college for permission to take the Senior Oxford Examination, which would qualify me to be a junior in college and thus eliminate three years. He thought this was very ambitious and an exaggeration of my capability because the current class was comprised of students who had already undergone two years of preparatory work. He felt that it was almost impossible to be on the same level with them. He also felt that if I should fail it would have a negative impact on the rating of the college. I convinced him that I would not fail, so I registered for the class.

My first few days in class were really challenging. I felt like a misfit and a lost sheep. In geometry, the class was studying theorem forty-nine, and I did not know how to do theorem one. My only hope was to claim the promise in Isaiah 40:31 that I just had to trust God, and He would help me to persevere despite the daunting task at hand. In algebra, they were doing quadratic equations, whereas I had never done algebra in any form. In order to understand these classes I had to study the basics on my own. In Spanish, they were doing conversational classes. I knew nothing about Spanish, and because they were so advanced, I took Latin by correspondence.

I had my Red Sea experience in English class. Although I had received distinction in English in my local exams, I had not done the advanced type I experienced during this first week. My first written assignment gave me the willies. When I went to the professor's office for my result, she held up my paper and said, "I am happy that you came because your work is a disgrace. You are totally stupid, ignorant, and too primitive to be in my class." Then she began to review my work again, and, with a red pencil, she underlined every sentence and almost every line and, with anger, repeated, "Needless of trying, you are unfit and are a disgrace to my class. Meet me in my office tomorrow so that I may send you to form IV where you belong." She dismissed me and slammed the door behind me.

In desperation, I shamefully bypassed my dormitory and all my friends and found an isolated spot on the farm. Placing my paper with its colored marking on the ground, I talked personally with the God who had helped me to survive the judgment of the obeah man. I poured out my burden to Him and told Him that I believed I could make it if He would help me. I then thanked Him for helping me.

Returning to my dormitory room I rewrote my paper, but the fear of failure dominated my mind, so I tore it up. The words "needless you try" raged in my mind. I wrote the paper again and again. The fear of failure was so strong that I tore it up and threw it in the trash can. I wrote it a third time, but this time I knelt and asked God for wisdom and the courage to hold on to my determination to make it. This time I did not destroy my work. The fear of failure had dissipated, and the will to succeed took over. The words "needless to try" still resonated, but I kept repeating, "I am going to make it; I can make it; I will make it." When we met the next day in English class, I handed in my work and took a seat in the back to avoid being recognized by the professor. The day passed, and I did not go to meet her as she demanded. The next day I again concealed myself in the rear of the classroom and watched as she demonstrated her fury in tossing workbooks all over the room with the words: "I am so disappointed in your work, what nonsense you have all done!" I was excited because I realized I was not alone. I was not the only "stupid one."

Then she said, "Only one young man has done something sensible. I want him to come up here and read what he has done, and when he is through I want you all to go to him and let him show you how to do it." Up until this time no one knew who it was until she called my name and I stood up. She herself was stunned. It was unbelievable, but from that day on, I was no longer the misfit, or the unknown. I quickly became the mentor and the model Senior Cambridge student.

If any man lacks wisdom, let him ask God for help, for He gives abundantly (see Romans 11:33). My self-esteem was at its highest, and I then saw my real self. My will to succeed far exceeded my fear of failure. By elimination time in April, the dean reassured me that I had no reason to fear because my credit rating was exceedingly high. By the end of the year, geometry, algebra, Latin, and all the other subjects had become easy for me. I had by then become the topic of discussion on campus. By exam time my confidence was so high I was completely relaxed throughout the entire day of testing. On the Friday afternoon when the results were announced, the student body was divided into two groups: those who thought I had passed the exam, and those who thought I had failed. . I recalled another of God's promises found in James 1:5. "If any of you lack wisdom, let him ask of God, that giveth to all men liberally." The positive group won—I passed the exam with excellent scores and made history on campus for surviving. Many of those I studied with failed, but God had blessed my efforts. Remember, if you are optimistic, you will see light where there is none. But you need to guard it because the pessimist will try to blow it out.

The next two years were rather interesting. I maintained a positive outlook in all my actions. I worked in the college bakery from 5 a.m. to 11 a.m. and attended classes from 1 p.m. to 6 p.m. I graduated with a 4.75 average and a cash credit to my account. Despite the negative comments of my English professor, I survived the negatives and made it.

There is a lot of room on the highway to success. There is room for you. You might have given up hope because the way seems to be so dark. Did you know that if you look up long enough you will see stars? They are telling you that there is hope ahead—just keep on pushing forward. You will be surprised to know that just around the corner is your source of strength—a loving, outstretched hand and a loving voice saying," I have been waiting for you. What took you so long?"

Don't give up. You are going to make it. Go for it. It is yours.

Chapter 3
Surviving Public Opinion
"Others have tried and failed."

It is a common tendency to see the failure of others who have tried as a justifiable reason for not trying. Failure in your predecessor offers you the opportunity to avoid doing that which accounts for his failure. The greatest failure in life is the failure to visualize why one fails.

When Columbus started out, he had no idea where he was going. When he arrived he did not know where he was, and when he returned he did not know where he had been. He had a goal and strove to achieve it, despite the negatives. He left the unpredictable to be interpreted by the pessimists. As a doctor I made my name by seeing patients who came to me after going to the most prominent physicians. I focus on avoiding repetitions. I generally do what my colleagues fail to do, and sometimes I do what to them was insignificant. Failures should be taken as steppingstones.

We at times set too low a value on ourselves, but we are made great or little by hard work and dedication. At twenty-four years of age I had finished college and was the headmaster of a primary school. By twenty-six I was a professor of three major subjects in a secondary school. At twenty-seven I was ordained as a minister of the gospel and had a parish of seventeen large churches. By thirty-three I had two homes, an expensive car, and four children. I was popular, progressive, and financially stable. I was a prominent executive, and to my colleagues, my employer, and my friends it was too great a risk to attempt fulfilling my ambition of becoming a physician. They all felt I had the potential, but my age, accomplishments, and social standing were a negative factor in pursuing a new career. To them, the shift from an independent,

Chapter 3 Surviving Public Opinion

accomplished family man to a student competing with young men and women was too great a risk.

For my employer, the vacuum that would be caused by my absence overrode his desire to see me become a physician. He had a long list of men much younger than I was, men with great ambitions but less achievements and stability who ventured to become physicians but got swept away by pressure and public opinion. He hated the very thought of me losing my social status and self-esteem because of the competitive pressure of medical school. He reminded me of the eight to ten years of relentless studying, the sacrifices, the expenses, and the stress on my family.

He was indeed a good man. I cherished his counsel because it was from a genuinely pure heart, but I knew the predicted difficulties. I saw the years of studying, the cost, the competitive age, and possible stress as challenges. I promised him that those were all useful steppingstones, and, with that in mind, I was prepared to break the circle by being the one who made it and returned to serve.

I am happy to say that twelve years later I returned as an accomplished physician and received a contract with him. It was a fulfilling reward to survive and break public opinion and the cycle of those who had tried and failed. By failing to prepare, we prepare to fail. Most of my colleagues eventually became my patients.

At forty-four I was a physician, and my three sons and one daughter were all enrolled in premed programs. By the time I turned forty-six, two of my children had received their degrees in medicine, one in dentistry and one in science.

One's motive for setting a goal can be a determinant to your achieving that goal. If you have a burden for money, in order to be rich you may be tempted to compromise some of your fundamental principles. If you are pressured by a deadline, you may be tempted to take shortcuts, which in most cases carries no guarantee. A bad time to plan a menu is when you are hungry. You may grab fast food instead of a balanced meal. Likewise a bad time to decide on a life career is when you are desperate for cash. Don't worry about the length of time it will take to achieve your goal—live one day at a time. Don't wait until you find the cash to meet the cost. The will to achieve must precede the way.

Don't worry about your future job. There is always an opening for an accomplished person suited for the job. The world is in search of men and women like you who have conviction. Don't lower your price. You can make it, and you will make it ... unless you choose not to make it.

When Hernando Cortez reached his destination, he burned his ships in an effort to convince his men that there was no turning back. In his ambition to conquer the world, Adolf Hitler destroyed bridges once he crossed them to show there is no about face. The will to succeed must exceed the fear of failure.

What is your burden at this time? Money to pay your bills? What are your plans? Well, there are some options.

- Worry about it. This will never pay it. It will cost you more with loss of sleep, loss of appetite, headaches, depression, and a possible nervous breakdown.
- Hide from your creditors. This will never clear it. It will cost you more. You will lose your credit for seven years. You may be evicted or have your salary garnished.
- Talk to your creditors. Let them see your financial plight and your willingness to meet your commitment.
- Make good on your promise. Remember, disgrace does not lie in the fall but in how long you remain down without getting up.

Are you searching for a job, a companion, or something else? You may need to change your approach, your attitude, or your methodology. Have you asked yourself the question, why am I not finding what I want? Do some personal evaluation and be willing to adjust.

The story is told of a traveler who got lost in a snowstorm. He struggled in the night to find a place of refuge. Late that night he stumbled into an object and fell. He felt so discouraged that he refused to get up and continue his struggle. He bundled up as best he could and suffered through the biting cold just to discover at dawn that he had slept right at the door of a cabin. Had he mustered up the courage to keep pressing on, he would have saved himself the bitterness of that cold wintry night.

You might be praying and looking for the answer but feel like heaven is silent. Don't give up. Keep pressing on. The darkest part of the night is generally the moment just before dawn. The night when I set the date for my wedding I knew I had no money and no new clothes. My pants and suits were all worn after years of pressing and dry cleaning, but I had prayed about it and was convinced that God would make a way out for me. I needed a companion because I was lonely. That very night a thief broke into my house and stole all my clothes.

My friends and employers sent me packages of new shirts, underwear, socks, kerchiefs, neckties, pants, suit material, and money. In exchange for my worn-out clothes, I got twice as much as I had, including new items and enough money to have suits made, including my wedding suit, and purchase a wedding ring for my fiancée.

If you are searching for direction, you need to turn to God because He knows the way through the wilderness. All you have to do is follow and trust Him with the outcome.

Chapter 3 Surviving Public Opinion

A young man in the middle of his last year in medical school received notice of a registered letter. Fearing it was from the school with bad news about his increasing indebtedness at the office, he avoided going to the office to sign for it. Being pressured for funds, he dropped out of medical school and after some time applied for a job at a laboratory where he had previously worked. He was shocked to be told that the executive committee had voted to assist him financially during his last year in school and had sent him the funds by registered mail. To his amazement, he recalled refusing to claim the letter, not knowing it carried the funds that he needed to finish medical school. It was too late. Because the funds had never been claimed, he lost his chance to graduate. The fear of failure had exceeded the will to succeed.

So many times we miss the mark because of fear and a lack of faith. I agree with a quote made by Ellen White, "you have nothing to fear for the future unless you forget what God has done in the past". I know that He is more than able to lead you through the future. So keep pressing on—you are going to make it if you choose to fight against adversities.

Chapter 4
Surviving Financial Pressure

"I wish I had the money" has become a universal saying. The pessimist capitalizes on it by saying, "Since you don't have the money, then don't try." Many plans have been cancelled and goals given up because of a lack of funds. Financial institutions take advantage of this and offer numerous promises to catch these unfortunate ones who, in their desperation, rush into traps. Sometimes we become too anxious and thus become captives of financial strains that end up as lifelong nightmares. This can also be one of the adversities that become a stumbling block in one's attempt to achieve. "How will I make it?" will always come up as soon as you contemplate making it. But if there is a will, there ought to be a way. Thus, finding the way will be determined by the strength of the desire to achieve.

Financial difficulties forced me to ask my employer for an increase in my salary. I did so because he was aware that although my performance was highly satisfactory, I was being underpaid. My request was not a demand, and it carried no threats. His response was threatening and insulting. My self-esteem was challenged to the extent that I saw it as an imposing issue. Should I be satisfied to continue under a financial situation that was unpredictable, or should I pursue my goal of becoming a physician? If I chose to pursue the latter, how would I make it? There were at least eight unpredictable years of training that I would have to face. I had financial obligations such as a mortgage payment on my home and my car, credit cards and other monthly payments, a wife and children in school. How would I make it? I prayed about it, and, realizing God knows the way, I decided to go to school.

Sometimes God allows unfavorable circumstances to come our way in order to move us to higher heights as is demonstrated in the following story.

Chapter 4   Surviving Financial Pressure

A fisherman encountered a bitter storm that destroyed his boat and left him stranded on an unoccupied island. He built a hut and merely survived for several days while he hoped desperately for some passerby to rescue him. One morning he decided to walk around the island. In his absence, his hut caught fire and was destroyed. This, he felt, was a curse from God, and he began to swear that God was unfair. It was not long before he heard voices. To his surprise, sailors from a passing ship told him they saw the smoke, which led them to realize someone might be in distress because the island was unoccupied.

God's ways are mysterious and may sometimes lead us to wonder, but if we follow Him, He will lead us through (see Romans 8:28).

My wife and I decided to make the trip to headquarters some 240 miles away to discuss my plans to attend medical school and to pick up my monthly paycheck. I needed counsel from my employer and was prepared to discuss the issue with an open mind with the hope that provision would be made so that I could continue working, even on a part-time basis, while going to school. At this stage I was not resistant to changes one way or the other.

Surprisingly, we were coldly received, and my employer became very adamant upon hearing my decision. He offered no encouragement, but laughingly shouted, "You will never make it. A short time ago you claimed you needed a raise in your salary because you were having difficulty making it, now you are here telling me about medical school. You are crazy and too ambitious; you'll never make it."

My wife responded, "As long as there is a God in heaven, he will make it."

He became more indignant and ordered his treasurer to hold my check. Then he told me I should consider myself fired. I appealed to him to reconsider his decision. He said it was an order, and I should go and advise my parishioners that I was fired. The 240 miles back were crowded with troubled thoughts. It was time for all my monthly bills to be met. When I reached home, I received a telephone call from my employer. He ordered me to bring in my car on Monday at 10:00 a.m., which was four days away. I told him I needed the car for school.

He said, "That's why I want you to bring it in."

I asked, "What if don't?"

He said, "You will regret it if you don't."

Circumstances had forced me to have him co-sign with me as security for my car. So unless I could stand alone without his signature, I had no choice but to surrender my car. My only option was to go back and seek help from God who had helped me so many times before. I sought a quiet spot in my office and pleaded with God. I prayed earnestly for help. On rising from my knees I had nothing to fear for the future unless I forgot how faithful God had been in helping me in the past. I met with all my creditors and explained my situation. I asked for extended time to meet my obligations. In response, they all complimented me on my determination to be a physician, and, as an incentive, they erased my debts and gave me certified receipts. A devout old lady, on hearing of my plight, invited me to pass by her home on my way to hand over my car. On reaching her home, she gave me a check to cover the balance on my car and advised me to park it in her garage. She had her chauffeur drive me to see my employer. I went straight to the bank that had financed my car, paid off the note, and retrieved the title. On reaching my employer's office, I told him the car was too heavy to take to his office, so instead I brought the title. He smiled and admitted it was useless trying to stop me. He wished me good luck.

Every road, especially the one that leads to higher heights, is decked with obstacles, or some unexpected problems. If you are determined to reach your goal, these challenges can be used as steppingstones. If circumstances deprive you of your wings, give God thanks for your legs because you are better off than the guy without legs.

Deprivation forces you to become a victim of circumstances, and if you are not careful, you will compromise your vision. Losing a job or even a loved one should not lead you to give up on God. If you believe in Him, then trust in His leadership. What He does not prevent, He allows for your own good. This philosophy is entrenched in the text that says, "All things work together for good to those who love God" (Romans 8:28). It is very difficult to appreciate loss as a favorable experience, but you can only be up or down. If you are losing, you're gaining faith in the future with God as your provider, which will help you to transform the negatives into positives.

> **If you choose to climb the mountains, then you will have to leave the valley.**

Within a short while, the news about my being fired became the talk around the city, and it aroused the interest of many sympathizers. Two prominent groups visited my home six days apart and offered to sponsor me through medical school and take care of my family. However, their demanding conditions were in conflict with my convictions, so I did not accept their offer.

The next two years during my premedical career were extremely hard and trying for my family and me. My wife worked during the day as a nurse, while I attended classes and worked nights as an orderly. There were days when my wife had to sell empty bottles in exchange for milk. The roads were very rough, the nights very dark, and the waters deep, but the star of hope kept twinkling in the distance, and He who has not broken a promise stood by us and led us through. The adjustment from being an aristocrat to being a peasant was a dilemma

Chapter 4 Surviving Financial Pressure

to many people, but to us it was a pebble on the highway that was leading us to a positive outcome.

I praise God for my wife and five children who stood by me and never flinched. We made it together and survived the financial pressures as a family. No one can successfully occupy two spaces at the same time. If you choose to climb the mountains, then you will have to leave the valley. The price of achieving success is sacrifice.

Chapter 5
Why So Ambitious

There is a feeling among some folks that certain careers or professions should be sought by people who are considered to be of the upper class. To them, this class is limited to the financially strong, those of a certain cultural group, the elite in society, or those with a strong family background. This philosophy can cause those who fall outside the above-mentioned circles to grope in the low places because to do otherwise would be seen as trespassing. Barriers in the form of criteria or prerequisites that are almost impossible to meet stand before them as if to say, "You are too ambitious, don't even try. You are heading in the wrong direction. The time frame is so long and the overall cost is so high. Your parents are not rich, and you just can't make it. Why are you so ambitious? Try something that takes less time and money." Because of these types of negative comments, potential first-class citizens have resorted to being satisfied with second or third class.

One early Monday morning as the children were filing in for the opening exercises of school, a mother who apparently was in great distress approached me in tears with her twelve-year-old son. He had been dismissed from his school because he was caught stealing. She pleaded earnestly for me to give him a chance in my school. He was her only child.

I approached the young man, and with my hand on his shoulder, I said, with a smile, "So, young man, are you a thief?"

He responded, "Yes, Sir, but I am willing to change."

I assured the mother that I would admit him and try to help him change according to his promise. I had previously announced that we would be selecting officers that morning for a Mother's Day Club. We needed a president, a vice president, a secretary, and a treasurer. When the time came for nominating a treasurer, I chose this young man. The whole school was astonished because he was not only the newest student but was known as a thief. Dues were collected that same morning, and with my permission, he, as the newly appointed treasurer, was put in charge of all funds. He was also commissioned to collect dues and was accountable to me.

In counseling the newly appointed officers, I gave an orientation of the duties of each one and admonished that they were to live up to the expectations of the student body. This young man stood up and remarked, "Teacher, my previous teacher told me I was a notorious thief. You, my new teacher, see me as an honest student and put me in charge of all this money. I thank you for giving me a chance to see myself, not as a thief, but as a trusted, honest student. I am going to do my best to live up to your expectations."

He kept his promise and was indeed a trusted and honest treasurer. He later graduated from the school of public health and became a chief public health inspector. In every man and woman there is hidden potential. Each of us should aim at reaching the moon with the determination that if we miss we will grab a star on the way down.

The story is told of two buckets that met at a well to draw water. One bucket complained, "This life is so miserable. Every time I leave the well full I come back empty."

The other bucket exultantly remarked, "This life is really exciting. Every time I come here empty I leave here full."

We are all in a world that is loaded with negatives and positives. Every man sees what he looks for.

I embrace the following statements:

Rough seas make good sailors.

Adversity is the pathway to success.

He who has never made a mistake has achieved nothing.

To illustrate these points, let me tell you a story.

I held some seminars for a prominent church. Among the participants was a prominent and wealthy physician. At the end of the sessions, he invited me to meet with him in his office. On arriving he complimented me for my eloquence, uniqueness, and preparedness. He offered me a contract to do a series of seminars for him. But I had been accepted to medical school and was scheduled to register for the first semester within two weeks. Thus, I expressed my regret that I could not take his contract. He enthusiastically tried to convince me that I was making a mistake in choosing a career in the medical field.

He said, "Have you considered what it costs to enter medical school? The books alone cost so much that you'll never make it. You are facing six to eight years of school, and each year the cost grows higher. One third of all students never make it through the first semester. Have you heard about anatomy, physiology, and biochemistry? Those subjects alone are hard enough to run you crazy. Then after medical school there is the internship. Son, that's where the rubber meets the road. Night duty alone will frustrate you. Then you'll have the State Board examinations, where you'll meet some of the toughest guys who are there to frustrate you."

Then he pointed his finger in my face and continued. "I have not told you the half of the story. You'll never make it. Why not be a nurse? It's easier, cheaper, and less nerve racking. Take some advice; you'll make a good nurse."

I smiled and said, "Sir, I did not come here to ask you if I can or will make it. I am here to let you know that I am going to make it, and I'll remind you about this conversation some day."

Four years later I received a call inviting me to give the official address for a church anniversary. I was sent a first class airline ticket, and to my surprise, the person who introduced me was the said doctor who advised me to be a nurse. He introduced me as Dr. R. E. Williams, a physician and lecturer. In his remarks he spoke of me as an example of someone who is determined to rise above the norm.

The world's greatest need today is for men and women who will stand by their conviction "as the needle to the pole" (Ellen G. White, *Education*, p. 57). It is a rewarding experience to look back and see the adversities you have survived in your struggle to achieve your goal. Choices may come in pairs or in multiples. The choice serves as a catalyst in the amount of enthusiasm you'll put out in making your choice a reality. Whenever one reaches toward his goal, he continually looks for an opportunity that enhances his achievement. He builds up immunity against negative thoughts and suggestions, and he presses forward in reaching his goal. He determines to not be distracted by the "you can't" or "you will not." Your chance to make it is right ahead of you, and there are only two things you can do: go for it, or give up.

A young man, upon finishing high school, approached his father's boss for a job on his farm. Instead, the good old farmer offered him a cow as a gift. He told him that the next day he would bring out his ten best cows and let the young man choose one by pulling on its tail as it passed by. The young man was filled with so much excitement that his anxiety kept him awake almost all night. He saw himself coming home with his cow and becoming a farmer in a few years with several heads of cows. He also saw himself as a cowboy riding his horse as he passed his cattle every day.

The next morning as he and his dad prepared for the great moment, he was advised to be calm and not be in a hurry in his selection. There would be ten cows passing by, and in most instances, the first ones might not be the best. The whole family was present to share in the excitement. The moment came, and the young man rolled up his sleeves as some robust, healthy Angus cows passed by. He almost grabbed the first one when he discovered that the succeeding one was bigger and looked much better than the first. After a few minutes more than half of the cows had passed by, and he realized that the best were yet to come. His mother shouted at him and asked him what he was waiting for. The eighth cow passed, and again it appeared much healthier than the preceding one. The ninth came by, but in his mind he felt that the tenth might be the best. Lo and behold, when the tenth passed he grabbed it, but it had no tail.

Opportunity is like the tenth cow without a tail. The best time to claim it is when it knocks, and the first knock you hear may be the last.

Procrastination is the thief of time. There is always a voice telling you to wait. It might say, "Wait until things are better. Why hurry? You still have a lot of time. If you miss this opportunity, you can always get another. Why worry? You can always do something else." Or it might be saying, "Give yourself a chance. Take it easy. Things will work themselves out."

Take a cue from nature. The woodpecker pecks until it bores a hole in the tree. A small termite chews through the foundation of the greatest mansion. It eats and eats, little by little, until one day the mansion falls. Your only hope of making it lies in your mind, not your financial status. You have what it takes to reach heights, but you have to start climbing bit by bit. You can be whatever you want to be, a sluggard or an achiever. The choice is yours.

One of the world's greatest achievers was Joseph, the hated son of Jacob. His brothers saw him as a dreamer, and because of jealousy they sold him as a slave. His master's wife accused him of sexual harassment and had him imprisoned. His prison companions saw him as an interpreter of dreams. And Pharaoh saw him as a ruler. Joseph rose to great heights because he used his misfortunes as steppingstones. His strength was founded in his willingness to refuse to allow what others thought of him to shape who he wanted to become (see Proverbs 3:5).

My supervisor told me I would never become a doctor, but because I refused to subject myself to her dictatorial, doggish attitude during my premedical studies, I made it. My organic chemistry teacher jokingly, but sarcastically, asked me if I thought I would make it. I seriously answered, "If I didn't think I would, I wouldn't have started."

Shortly after I started, my brother, who had promised to help me, advised me to give up because the climb was too steep. My reply to him was, "I have started, and I will not turn back." He later became one of my patients.

Consider this illustration: A ship responded to a distress call from another ship. "What is your problem?" the first ship asked.

The captain shouted, "We are out of water!"

"Let down your buckets, you are sailing on the Amazon River," was the reply.

The world is full of opportunities. If you listen to your instinct and search for the One who created you, you'll find fulfillment. Remember, God even cares for the sparrows. You are included in His budget. You have a share in His bounties—why not claim it? "Trust in the Lord with all your heart, and lean not on your own understanding" (Proverbs 3:5, 6). They that trust in Him shall want no good thing. He will make your wishes come true (see Psalm 1).

> **Don't allow circumstances to force you to compromise your ambition.**

Don't allow circumstances to force you to compromise your ambition. When the way is obscured by uncertainties, don't give up. Keep looking to God who is still the same yesterday, today, and tomorrow. Keep looking up; He will not fail you. Discouragement has frustrated many, but you don't have to follow the norm. Just be yourself, and be the person you want to be. Don't lower your price tag. Your opportunity is on its way and will soon be passing within reach. It may be delayed, but it will be worth it, just wait and see.

Chapter 6
Surviving Counterfeits

It is a general tendency to accept a professor's statement as indisputable based on his experience as a teacher. It is of particular concern when such remarks are made on the first day of class. Students are all curious and will, by the end of the period, form impressions of the teacher. Some are hesitant to dispute his statement with the fear that it may impact their final grade.

As an introduction to psychology, our professor gave us an IQ test in our first class. Nobody knew it was an IQ test, but after taking it, the professor announced that no one who made less than 70 percent would pass his class. That statement came as a shock because more than half of the class had made less than 60 percent. I, too, was shocked as I scored 65 percent.

In a split second, I saw the picture. Here was a man telling me in plain words that I was not going to make it. Why then should I take his class? I would be wasting valuable time. He was telling me that no matter how hard I studied I would still fail his class. I took the courage to raise my hand for permission to speak. All eyes were now focused on me. "Sir, with all due respect, I am challenging your statement. The only reason why I am in this class is to make an A, and unless you deliberately fail me, I am going to make it."

He said smiling, "I appreciate you challenging my statement because I did not intend to intimidate anyone. I was hoping it would give you the courage to challenge it." I finished his course with an A.

You must be willing to face challenges. Counterfeits are deceptive, and they are intended to weaken your appreciation for things that are real. The sources of counterfeits may enhance your acceptance, but do not be deceived, they are wolves in sheep's clothing. If you are in a battle, you need to fight with all your might, regardless of the surrounding casualties, because your whole life depends on it. You will never reach the East if you are heading West. You have to set your priorities in the right place. You are as big as you think you are, because the mind is the measure of the man.

The person who is afraid to start never arrives. You need to become acquainted with yourself and realize that one of the biggest factors in you reaching your goal is your thinking. On most highways there are bridges, some narrow, others wide. There may be corners, some are dangerous while others are not. There will be dangerous, careless drivers, wild animals, police officers, bad weather, and a lot of unpredictable things. When you are traveling, it would be poor strategy to focus only on the unpredictable things. The feeble mind magnifies the negatives; the positive mind sees the destined goal, despite the pitfalls, the dangers, and the unpredictable things. Fears build phobias, which in turn create impassable roadblocks. Fear is a close companion to doubt, whose counterpart is frustration. This is the highway that leads to depression. A depressed person is paranoid, suspicious, and loses the will to fight.

No one is immune to fear and doubt, but everyone has the potential to generate the power of positive thinking. Fear always conceals confidence. When you believe you can do it, then you are on the road to developing how to do it. No one will live long enough to find a highway without some obstacles; therefore, we must be prepared to find our way through the unpredictable. Rough seas make good sailors; disappointment and problems make good survivors.

A few months after I was fired from my job, a tornado destroyed my car. I was then carrying two jobs while enrolled in my premed classes. I could not afford insurance on my car. Ironically, my car was the only one in the crowded parking lot that was destroyed. Mockingly, my employer jeered at me and said, "Christianity is no help to you." I told him that quite likely I was the only target for the evil one. There upon I called a wrecker to take my car to the nearest body shop. The next day the manager called for my insurance to start working on my car. I told him I did not have any insurance, but he should hurry up and finish my car because his money was guaranteed.

Ten days later I received a call telling me that my car was ready. I only had 25 cents, which was enough to take the bus to the body shop. Before leaving for the bus stop, I went into the bathroom and talked to God. I told Him the mere fact that He did not prevent the damage to my car was evidence that He would take care of the repairs. I told Him I had enough confidence that He would. I gave Him thanks and left for the shop. It was a challenging thought, but I believed and acted on my belief. Honestly, I wished the trip to the body shop had been longer, but it was a very short one. On arriving at the garage, I said, "Lord, my car is ready and is in the shop. I'm going for it."

As soon as I disembarked from the bus, someone yelled at me from across the street. It was an old woman who had heard me preach and to whom I had

Chapter 6   Surviving Counterfeits

sold some books. She invited me in and asked why I was riding the bus. I related to her the whole story. My car had been destroyed by the tornado two weeks ago. I had brought it to the body shop next door. Now it was ready, and I was on my way to pick it up.

"Were you insured?" she asked.

"No, Ma'am, I was not."

"Then how are you going to pay for it? Do you have the money?"

"No, Ma'am, I am trusting God, and I know He will keep His promise."

"Do you really believe that God is going to take care of it?"

"Yes, Ma'am, I really do."

"I am impressed," she said. Then she asked, "Do you have time to go down to the bank?"

"Yes, Ma'am, I do," I replied.

Amazingly, she gave me a check to cover the total cost of the repairs, plus insurance for one full year. *I believe that belief is progressive.* It first leads you to believe in yourself. Then it fosters belief in people and then belief in a superior being who is capable of leading, protecting, and maintaining anyone who believes in Him.

Belief is a catalyst that generates accomplishment because one sees in us what we see in ourselves. We are products of our thoughts. No one will believe in you until you believe in yourself. Your friends will capitalize on your misfortune in an effort to discourage and frustrate you, but remember, one sees in life what he looks for. One who earnestly looks for success generally finds it. To the positive mind, a glass that is half empty is half full.

Here's another illustration. A young man, upon arriving at a train station, discovered he had missed his train by ten minutes. In disgust, he remarked, "I just did not drive fast enough." To his surprise, a bystander who heard him remarked, "You just did not start on time."

It is natural to blame circumstances for our failures. To achieve your goal, you must make up your mind to not allow yourself to be deceived or to believe in the counterfeit messages out there that try to dissuade you from success.

Negative messages are intended to look like the real thing, and unless you know what the real thing looks like, you will be misled. The fingers of a banker are trained to know the touch of good money so that when a counterfeit comes along his finger readily recognizes it. Thus, he does not waste his time studying the counterfeit because he recognizes that it is far more practical knowing the genuine article. Set your face toward your goal, and the counterfeit messages will fall out of your way.

Chapter 7
Surviving the Impossible

Have you ever come to a point in your life where you felt it was impossible to make it? Have you ever felt like you've tried every available resource without success, and now with certainty you build up such hope in the last one only to fail again? Consider this story.

Two men were caught stealing sheep. They were tried and sentenced to be branded in the forehead with the acronym S.T., meaning sheep thief. One felt that since he was branded it was irrevocable, so he continued stealing sheep. The other felt that despite public opinion he would endeavor to change his lifestyle. He managed to get a job as a tourist guide. Years went by, and while leading a group, someone curiously asked another guide what the S.T. meant. The person answered, "I have seen it for such a long time but never asked." About five minutes passed, and he returned to the questioner. With a smile he said, "I think it is the abbreviation for a saint."

Remember that with God all things are possible, and man's extremity is God's opportunity. He has promised that however deep the waters they will not overcome you. When the way you are traveling becomes so dark that you cannot see, it's time to look up, for there is a star hidden under the cloud. You may not see it at a glance, but if you keep looking up, it is there for you. The God who loves you so much that He gave His only son to die for you would rather strip heaven of every angel to lead you through (see Isaiah 43:2–4).

It is always so rewarding to trust in Jesus and His Word. *It is very encouraging to know God has never left anyone to suffer in the dark.* He led the children of Israel through the Red Sea, through the Jordan River, and then through the wilderness for forty years. No one among the thousands of Israelites had a bank account or any income, but He provided enough for them on a daily basis for 14,400 days.

You need to convince yourself that He cares for you and if you trust Him He will provide. During my second year in medical school I became an advocate for a student who had a conflict with a faculty member. Later on, that faculty member became my teacher for physiology. He didn't appear to hold any grudges against me for advocating for the other student, that was, until I took the final exam and left for summer break. On returning I discovered that I had failed the exam and would have to repeat the class. Fortunately, a fellow classmate who had taken the exam with me met me and told me with a smile that I had passed the exam because he had seen the list. This story didn't match up with the fact that the teacher said I had failed.

I was facing the possibility of losing one year of school. My friend agreed to go with me to see the director of the university who had my file. Upon meeting with him it was clear that my grade had been changed from an A to an F. Thankfully, he ordered the restitution of the original grade, and I gladly started my third year of medical school. To all my friends, this was surviving the impossible. It had never been done. There were others who had been equal victims of similar circumstances, but feeling that it was impossible to dispute such decisions, they had taken the path of least resistance. For me, this was another case that challenged my faith. The nearer I came to achieving my goal, the more challenges I encountered.

> **We should not blame our failures on "bad luck." Instead, we should seize the opportunity to learn from our mistakes and use them as steppingstones.**

I needed to be reminded that *the closer one comes to the mountaintop, the steeper and harder the climb.* I was totally committed to achieving my goal because there were too many who thought I could not. I learned through these experiences that once the barking dog recognizes one to be a friend he stops barking and wags his tail. I became the untouchable because my enemies recognized that I knew how to undo their knots. Remember, one has reason to fear for the future when he forgets the miracles of the past.

It is very easy to allow our uncultured situations to conquer us. On the other hand, in the crowded world of success, there are those who have overcome tough situations, but it all has to do with their response to defeat. It lies in the art of bouncing back, learning a lesson, forgetting the defeat, and moving on. Your persistence should forbid you from seeing yourself as defeated. It is a matter of gaining from failures instead of losing through frustrations. Our encounters with opposition, discouragement, setbacks, or personal misfortunes should become steppingstones to propel us forward.

One's reaction to failure should provide a clue to one's potential for success. Setbacks are valuable learning tools. We should objectively look in the mirror and see if we are what we really think we are and be bold enough to take corrective measures if necessary. Being self-critical can be constructive in helping one to build the basic skills necessary for success. We should not blame our failures on "bad luck." Instead, we should seize the opportunity to learn from our mistakes and use them as steppingstones.

The light bulb is the result of thousands of experiments, but the founder, in his persistence, learned from each failure. If you believe in yourself, then reach for your goal and stick with it. Something becomes impossible only when you think it is impossible. You need to convince yourself that you can survive the impossible. A person generally sees what he looks for. Begin looking for possibilities, and you will find it easy to survive the impossibilities.

There are a lot of circumstances that God could prevent, but He permits them to prove to the devil that you can cope without failing. Thus, when we fail, we allow the evil one to commercialize on our failure. Jesus hesitated when He got the message from Mary that Lazarus was seriously ill. Had He immediately traveled to their home, in fulfillment of Mary's wish, Lazarus would not have died, but then one of the greatest miracles of His ministry would not have taken place. Going there when all hope had disappeared led to greater joy and deeper satisfaction because having been dead for four days made the extension of life a richer and more enjoyable experience (see John 11). *We must learn to appreciate life's complexities because it takes the darkness of night to help us enjoy the light of day. With God all things are possible.*

Chapter 8
Surviving the Ultimate
Time Is Against You

There are occasions in traveling when you come to a dead end. On the road it may read "No Outlet." Thus, your only way out is to turn around. In business, it may be a collapse, and your only option is to file bankruptcy. In school, it might be a failed class or financial challenges. For me it ran into financial problems when I had only six weeks left in medical school. It was at this time that I received the following letter from the financial director.

Dear Robert,

According to our records, you owe the school four hundred and fifty dollars. This serves to advise you that unless this is paid off within 21 days, you will not be allowed to sit for your final exams.

My family and I were seated at dinner when the mail arrived. It was a real shock to everybody. My wife dropped her fork, and the children all lost their appetite. I got up from the table, and with the letter still opened, I went into the nearby bathroom. Kneeling down with the letter, I read it out loud to God. I thanked Him for bringing me this far. I told Him that I needed $450, and I needed it soon. I said, "Thank you, Father, for being so kind." I then went back to the table and finished my dinner.

My wife, in distress, said, "Honey, what are you going to do? Where you are going to get $450 in three weeks? Do you mean that you can't graduate?"

In response, I said, "Honey, I talked it over with my Father, and He said it would be okay."

During the night, my wife was restless, and upon waking me, she remarked, "Honey, how can you be sleeping when your whole career is at stake?"

I reminded her that I had talked with my Father about it, and I had no reason to be worried. I reassured her that everything would be okay. The next day I went to class as usual. On reaching home, the prevailing question was, "Daddy, anything new?" My answer was, "Not yet." Two days went by, and I still did not know how God was going to work it out. On the third day, the mailman brought a letter that brightened my hopes. It was from a gentleman who I had never met in person. I had talked with him sometime previously and had his word that he would get in touch with me soon. It went like this:

> *Robert, I am doing my income tax returns, and you came across my mind. Please reply early and let me know if there is anything I can do for you.*

My wife, upon reading the letter, was excited but felt that it would be too bold to ask him for so much money. I answered, smiling, "I am going to ask him for the exact amount." My reply went like this:

> *Dear Mr. _____,*
>
> *Your letter came three days after I had been given 21 days to pay off a bill of $450 or else I will not be allowed to graduate. I would really appreciate your check of $450. Thanks in advance for your favorable and early reply.*

Within seven days, I received a certified letter with a cashier's check for $450. So many times, when we hear or read stories of extraordinary experiences, we consider such miracles as only happening to extraordinary people. We pray for rain but forget to stop the leaks in the roof or clean the gutters. We feel free to ask God for enough for groceries, but we go to the bank or our friends for $10,000 or $100,000. We consider some things too enormous to seek God's help.

A young man was delegated to represent his church at a world conference. On arriving at the conference center, he budgeted the few dollars he had in his billfold and discovered that he had enough money to buy some crackers and cheese to survive the ten-day conference session. For three days he had crackers and cheese three times per day. On the fourth as he was about to go for his regular crackers and cheese, a fellow delegate showed him a menu for the day and asked him if he was going to the dining room. He said he wished he could, but he did not have the money to purchase any meals. His friend was amazed and began to laugh.

"Why are you laughing?" the young man asked. "Is that funny?"

"Yes, it is funny because you said you don't have the money to buy your meals. Didn't you know that your meals are included in the price of your ticket?

They have all been paid for."

In disgust, he said to himself, "I have been living all these days on crackers and cheese when all my meals have been paid for."

Our genetics, nationality, or social backgrounds have nothing to do with our survival. God sees you as an individual, not a group. He has enough in His budget to meet your individual needs, regardless of what they may be. Needs are variables, and no two persons' needs are likely to be the same. Money may be the number one need for some.

One morning as I entered the hospital to do my regular morning rounds, the receptionist asked if I had a few minutes to talk with her. She asked with some hesitation, "Dr. Williams, what is it that makes you so pleasant? You are always smiling, and you seem to always be happy? We have been talking about you, and some of us have decided that it is either because you are very rich or you have no problems."

To this I replied, "You guessed right. I am rich."

She jumped up and, with a shout, said, "I knew it. I knew it. I knew that you had to be very rich to be so pleasant and so nice."

Then I quoted a phrase from one of Harriet Buell's hymns: "My father is rich in houses and lands, He holdeth the wealth of world in his hands, of rubies and diamonds, silver and gold, His coffers are full He has riches untold. I am a child of a King."

This is the status we all have the privilege to enjoy. If your Father is rich and you are an obedient child, then you ought to go about with a pleasant countenance. You will not complain, be fretful, or depressed. Wherever I go, people always assume that I am rich because of the way I carry myself with self-confidence and a smile. It is not the price of the clothes you wear that makes you great, but rather the person in the clothes that sets the price.

Should you be out shopping for a car, a pair of shoes, a dress, or a suit, don't start out at the bargain counter. Start at the most expensive counter. By this move, you will attract attention and service because self-service does not merit attendant service. Wherever there is a crowd, things are going cheap. You are ten times better off being assumed rich than being considered poor. Your first impression is generally your most convincing impression. Always be at your best.

Endeavor to be remembered by your pleasing personality, your winning profile, your realness, your positive approach, and your dynamic looks. People like to do business with clients who are winsome, pleasant, positive, and businesslike in their appearances. A prince should be easily recognized without having to tell his onlookers that he is a prince. His behavior, speech, and personality should display his status in whatever situation he finds himself.

As a struggling survivor, your greatest need may be a good paying job comparable to your experience. You might be having sleepless nights because you have been searching unsuccessfully for a job. It can be quite disturbing when daily necessities cannot be met because of a lack of funds. Bills may be piling up, collectors may be calling every day, and sometimes just a few dollars would be enough to meet the demands. I recall days when I would have felt rich if I only had one dollar in my pocket. A morsel is sweetest when eaten by someone who is starving. A dollar is a lot to someone who is broke, as is a job to someone who is destitute. It was at a time like this that I got a call from an old friend informing me that someone wanted my address because he had a job for me. It was a job that exceeded my expectations. Sometimes we give up a few minutes too early, as is evident in the following story.

A young man began to blame God for his problems. He had been searching without success for a job for several months. His pastor visited him and found him at the point where he contemplated taking his life because he had lost everything by foreclosure. He felt there was no real God because he had been praying for months without any evidence that He was hearing. The pastor reassured him that God's resources were inexhaustible and that faithfulness in all services to Him qualified one for His resources.

The young man went home, and after serious thinking, decided to reconcile with his service to God and his church. He discovered that he had not been faithful in paying his tithes and decided to make amends. What he had in his checking account was far less than what he owed, but he withdrew it and brought it to the pastor. The surprised preacher assured him that God had promised He would pour out more than he could consume. In disbelief, the young man replied that in no way could that be a reality because he was so destitute of so many things that he could not get more than he needed. That very night he received two letters in his mailbox, and each of them was an offer for a job that would start the following Monday morning.

Curiously enough, he could only accept one. He surely had more than he could manage. Waiting is always accompanied by anxiety. The hours always seem twice as long, even more so when you are waiting to get a call or a letter or an e-mail about a potential job offer. Anxiety is maximized and tolerance seems to fly away in this type of situation. Faith in God is not like dealing with the immigration department where you are dealt with according to the date and time when your application is received. Because Jesus lives, you can face tomorrow and be assured He is there to help you when you need it most (see Matthew 6:31).

Some time ago I had a scheduled meeting for 7:00 p.m. at one of my churches. That day I had an emergency that called me out of town, and I did not reach the church until midnight. The members confessed that because I had never missed an appointment with them they were prepared to keep on singing even until daybreak because they were confident I would come.

God has an unbroken record of being faithful in keeping His promises. You may have to wait a long time, but just keep on believing: He will answer your prayer. While you are waiting, it may be worthwhile to review your goals. If you are looking for a job, when was the last time you updated your curriculum vitae? Have you considered a temporary job while you are waiting? While I was waiting for my license, I took a temporary job washing bottles for a bottling company. My fellow workers on the job were alcoholics. The language was distasteful, but the mind is the measure of the man, and I knew why I was there. Working among them and for minimum wage did not change my personality. It was a temporary situation. It was not long before the management recognized my status and wanted me to work in the office, but I knew what I wanted and was satisfied to continue on a temporary basis.

I know of a young man who has been without a job for years because he has not succeeded in getting the job he wanted. If you have been waiting for a very long time, you may want to pursue an online course or do some voluntary service to update your experience. Whatever you do, please don't give up. Keep pressing on; things will change for the better. Remember, there are only two directions in which you can go: up or down. If you are presently down, the only other option for you is going up. It is during this time that stress escalates, the demands for funds multiply, and the waiting lists grow longer. The longer the waiting time, the shorter your work experience grows. I propose that one does not need to sit down and grope in the dark because the electricity is out when you can light a candle, a lamp, or a torch.

Opportunities are always passing by. You have to grab one because it may not return. It might not be the opportunity you were dreaming of, but it will suffice until your dream job comes along.

For example, a young man applied for a job as a manager. Although he was highly qualified, the vacancy was already filled, so he accepted the only available opening as a security officer. He exhibited such high ideals that it was not long before he was promoted to chief security officer. This was not his area of expertise, but he took every opportunity to learn the job and did such an excellent job that in less than eighteen months when the job for which he had previously applied became available he was offered the position without hesitation. When aiming for the moon, you should be ready to grab a star if by chance you failed to reach the moon.

In the parable of the ten talents as told by Jesus, the only man who was not promoted was the one who received one talent because he became dormant waiting for more opportunities to come his way before he started (see Matthew 25:14–26). He overlooked the fact that it is quality that counts, not quantity. You should be flexible and adaptable so that you will be willing to accept what you cannot change. Remember, the same vessel that is half empty is half full.

Perhaps you have been looking for a job for a long time. Don't give up. Review, revise, and strategize your methods. Convince yourself that you will survive any adversity that might be sent your way. It may be that your goal is to find a companion to be your wife or husband. If you have been searching for a considerably long time, then it may be about time you revise your expectations. Sometimes the features you are expecting in your Eve or Adam are too high. It is very difficult to find a perfect prefabricated companion.

If you set wealth as a number one factor in your choice, you may succeed in inheriting luxury that is devoid of true love, tolerance, and caring that enhance happiness and longevity. Beauty is only skin deep and may camouflage the ideals that are fundamental for a happy home. It would be helpful to do a self-evaluation by standing before a mirror and envisioning yourself in comparison to the person that your Adam or Eve is looking for. How do you measure up? Your profile, your personality, your physique, your appearance—are they at their best? Do you meet the criteria of a good companion? What will it take to bring that person in the mirror to be the one that is being sought for?

Furthermore, you may need to change where you are looking. The possibility may rest in your making some visits to other congregations, conventions, social gatherings, or educational institutions. As you interact with others, endeavor to be the ideal Adam or Eve that someone is praying and looking for. Don't be over anxious or else you may be irrational in your decision-making ability. Your companion may need some final touches to be what you really want, but your tender loving care will create the blend that helps living together an Eden on earth. Wealth achieved together enhances longer and deeper love than luxury achieved otherwise. Remember, a home is not made of bricks, carpet, expensive cars, and luxurious furnishings. A home is founded on love, patience, care, and a mutuality that solicits growing, living, eating, planning, talking, and sleeping together. To find such togetherness, one has to be focused and selective because the wrong choice will lead to lifelong discord, frustration, distress, anxiety, and misery. Good things come to those who wait. Don't be in a hurry, and don't give up. There is someone somewhere searching and waiting for you. You can survive this adversity.

It may be that your primary need is just to have a little more money to meet your basic needs. By the time the major bills are paid, there is hardly any money left to provide lunch money for the children, gas for the family car, or funds for unexpected emergencies. These may be included in the package of all the needs God promises to supply according to His riches in glory, which I have experienced in my life.

I had just been transferred to a new district, and the moving expenses had depleted all my available funds, resulting in no food in the house. It was Friday,

Chapter 8 Surviving the Ultimate

and I was in the backyard washing the family car. About sixty yards away was an open slaughterhouse, and the carcass of a slain cow could be seen hanging from a hook. The helper had just reported to my wife that she had nothing to prepare for dinner. My wife, in turn, came and told me that there was no food in the house and the children were hungry. I looked at her and, with a sigh, said, "Why not tell it to your heavenly Father. I am only your husband, and I don't have any money."

She saw the butchers cutting beef and, with an equally deep sigh, remarked, "I would surely enjoy a piece of that beef. It looks so good."

Have you ever had a feeling that leaves you guilty, inadequate, incompetent, and insufficient? That was how I felt when she spoke the second time. Again, I said, "Go tell it to Jesus." Evidently she did, because shortly after she began helping me clean the inside of the car, she excitedly showed me a silver dollar she had found in the crevices of the car seat. I told her to keep on looking because there might be more. Unbelievably, she kept searching and succeeded in finding enough between the other seats to purchase three pounds of beef.

While our helper went to purchase the beef, my wife responded to a knock at the gate. To her surprise, a member of the church greeted her with a huge basket of fruits and farm products, including yams, potatoes, onions, bananas, breadfruit, eggs, and vegetables. She told us that she and her husband had felt compelled to fix us the package and bring it at that time. Not knowing us well enough, she said she hoped we could find some use for what she brought. No wonder Jesus advised us to take no thought or worry about our food or clothing (see Matthew 6:31).

God provides enough for the birds; He has more than enough to supply your needs. He was willing to die for you. You don't have to be an Elijah or a great evangelist to receive His blessings, just be yourself and acknowledge Him as your Father, and as His child, tell Him your needs. He will provide. Remember, man's inadequacy is God's opportunity, and with His help, you can survive any adversity, such as my journey to Mexico.

Going to Mexico was not only an exciting experience but also an adventure. I had already been to two prominent medical schools but was introduced to a school in Mexico. The name Guadalajara spelled excitement and aroused my enthusiasm of immersing myself in Spanish culture. A friend and his family decided to make the 1,800-mile trip with me. This began a series of challenging experiences. Our first challenge came 1,200 miles away when we reached the border. Everything went smoothly until we reached the *aduana /adejuana* (checkpoint) twenty miles in from the border. I was refused entry because my passport had expired. The border guards told me to go back to San Antonio, which was 200 miles away, to get a new passport.

I knew that it would take longer than two or three days to get my passport renewed. I wondered if this was a sign that I should not enter Mexico. Thereupon, I decided to talk to God about it. I resorted to a nearby restroom, and on my knees I opened my expired passport and asked God to allow me entrance into Mexico if it was His will for me to go to school there. I thanked Him and started back for the immigration office. As soon as we approached the checkpoint, the same officer who had sent us back met me and shouted, "Are you back?"

I answered, "Yes, sir."

Without hesitating, he said, "Go ahead."

You should have been there to see the excitement as we drove into the heart of Mexico. Everybody was incredibly happy. I had received proof that it was God's will for me to go to school in Mexico.

My second challenge came on arriving in Guadalajara. I did not know any Spanish, so I had difficulties finding the right school. I communicated solely by sign language and that sometimes was very misleading. I ended up in the wrong school, and when I tried to register, they told me I could not apply because I was not a national. In my frustration, I resorted to a nearby park to talk to God again. I thanked Him for bringing me into Mexico and revealed to Him my predicament. I pleaded with Him for help. I was like a lost sheep needing someone to lead me to the right school. It was a challenging task, but I knew He was up for the challenge. He had done it for me the day before at the border, and I was asking Him to do it again. I gave Him thanks and sat up.

In less than five minutes a young man who happened to have been a member of one of my churches and for whom, many years before, I had served as a reference, walked up to me and shouted, "Pastor Williams, what in the wide world are you doing here?" He told me that he had just arrived back in town. He said, "You must have been praying because I kept wondering why I was going to the park?" On explaining my plight, he took me to the school. It was his alma mater, and it took him but a few minutes to get me registered.

I am a child of God, and His banner over me is love. He knows the way; He has the answer to every question and the solution to every problem. If you have had experiences of survival, they should serve to reinforce and reassure you that you are on the way to achieving your goal, despite the barriers of life. If you have been struggling and cannot, with certainty, confirm or identify divine intervention, then talk to those who have tangible experiences of divine intervention when human efforts have failed and lean upon them.

My next challenge came during the registration process. I had to pay my registration fee plus my first semester tuition, and I knew I did not have that amount in my bank in Texas. I did not anticipate all these expenses. My friend warned me that a bounced check is a federal crime in Mexico. I assured him my check was safe. I was now faced with the challenge of beating the check home. We hurried back home to Texas, and my next prayer to God was one of gratitude for His help in all my accomplishments and for His endorsement to register at school through my chance encounter with a former church member. I also asked Him for funds to clear the check that I had issued to the school. On arriving home I gave my wife the incredible news that I was registered in medical school and that I had paid my first semester tuition.

"Where did you get the money from?" she asked.

I answered. "I have not gotten it yet."

I hurriedly went to my post office box, and, in answer to my prayer, there was a letter with a check that was just enough to cover the check I had issued.

Challenges, challenges, challenges. Life is full of them. *God delights in meeting challenges.* He said, "Call upon Me in the day of trouble; I will deliver you, and you shall glorify Me" (Psalm 50:15). When you pass through deep waters, He will be with you to save you from drowning. He is a good lifeguard. When stress envelops you like a furnace, He promises to be with you so you will not be consumed with depression. He is a good fireman. He saved Daniel's three friends from an oven that was so hot the men who threw them in were consumed by the heat, whereas the three Hebrews did not experience loss of even a single hair. Only the rope that bound them was consumed (see Daniel 3:19–27). *It is a rich experience learning* to *trust in One who is reliable, dependable, and trustworthy.* I really enjoy such a relationship. It guarantees my surviving any adversity.

The history of the Israelites in Egypt is enlightening. They had been slaves for many years. They were now tired and homesick for freedom. To them, freedom had become a fantasy, but the story says that they cried unto God for deliverance, and He heard their cry. From slavery to freedom meant traveling from Egypt to Canaan. As they traveled, they came to the Red Sea, at which point they became trapped between the sea and the approaching Egyptian army. God heard their cries, and the Red Sea parted. They safely crossed over to the other side on dry land (see Exodus 14:26–31). Regardless of what your Red Sea is, when God hears your cry, it will become dry land. You do not have to become a saint to call on Him. Just as you are, wherever you are, whoever you are, you can call on Him and He promises He will answer.

Life is full of uncertainties and unpredictable events that threaten to overtake us like a flood, but if we call on Him, He promises to rise up a standard against them. One time I had an employee of mine go downtown and create some exorbitant bills in my name. On learning that I had contested the bills, he became bitter and, in revenge, made plans to kill me. But on his way to my house, he got into a conflict with another man and was stabbed and rushed to the hospital. When I learned of his injury, I visited him at the hospital. Shortly thereafter he was discharged and was waiting for a taxi to take him home. He was astonished when I offered to take him home in my car. He asked if I had heard about his plot to kill me, and on learning that I had, he marveled at my coming to look for him and my willingness to take him home. He admitted it must have been some divine intervention on my behalf because he was determined to take revenge on me. He apologized and pleaded for the chance to continue working for me.

Don't be discouraged; by His grace you will survive adversities. Remember that your heavenly Father has assigned you a guardian angel to watch over you. I have so many stories where my angel has intervened and saved my family and me. The following story is just one more example.

After sleepless nights of studying, I took my final exams and began the journey home for semester break. Traveling eastward, the morning sun kept striking me in my face, and I felt sleepy. Being the sole driver in the family, I pulled over on a side road to rest. Simultaneously, a red Falcon car pulled up parallel to me. I looked at the driver of the other car and told my wife I did not feel safe going to sleep with this guy beside me. I decided to leave. As soon as I started the car, he held up a gun and asked me where I thought I was going. I responded, "Nowhere," and sped off. Luckily, as soon as I entered the highway, I was able to intercept two buses and escape being trailed by the gunman. I was so scared that all fatigue had vanished.

> **Divine intervention is not a fable. Living, personal experiences have made it a proven fact.**

My wife and children were all overwhelmed with fear and kept looking back for the red car. They all insisted I remain between the two buses until we reached the next city. It was later announced over the radio that travelers should be on the lookout for a dangerously armed, escaped prisoner in a red Falcon car.

Divine intervention is not a fable. Living, personal experiences have made it a proven fact. You can prove it by calling on Him wherever you are and wait for His caring answer. Be assured that with His help you can and will survive any adversity

Chapter 9
Surviving Trends

There are trends that seem to become a pattern to the extent that they seem to be accepted as the norm. One of the major concerns expressed by my employer when I told him of my plans to pursue medicine was that he was afraid I would be like many others who had left but not returned after they had achieved their goal. He mentioned that everyone who left to take up medicine chose to stay in the country where they got their degree.

In my travels I encountered a number of individuals from my homeland of Jamaica. I was always so excited to meet them. One of my first questions was, "What part of the island are you from?" Without exception, everyone claims to have been born in Kingston, the capital. For some reason, one never admits to being born in the country. It is a fact that some in truth were from Kingston, but why should one conceal the fact of their birthplace in the country? Is it because everybody knows or hears about the city and it saves you the trouble of telling someone where your hometown is located? Or is it that you are ashamed to admit you were born in the country and not in the city?

During a conversation with a fellow countryman, I asked him when was the last time he had been back home. He told me it was some three years ago. He said he would be happy to visit more frequently, but life in the country was not what it used to be and he had a hard time adjusting to an "outdated" sort of life again.

I was born in a little village four miles from the nearest town. The roads were gravel. There was no electricity, no water pipes, and no telephone system. I was accustomed to taking baths in a tub, using an outhouse, and cooking meals over a wood fire. I had to walk four miles to school and was whipped with a strap if I was late. I had to show deep respect to all elderly people by saying "Yes, sir" or "Yes, ma'am."

There was no house-to-house mail delivery, and the nearest post office was four miles away.

Life in those days, however, was a thrilling one. I was satisfied with what we had and followed a healthier lifestyle by eating fresh fruits and vegetables from the garden. The crowing rooster was my timekeeper, and the whistling birds my musicians. There were no parks, no movies, and no bus service, so I played in our backyard, listened to a battery-run radio, and rode a donkey or walked to our destinations. However illustrious my present manner of living may be, to me, it cannot be compared to the tranquility and the happiness I enjoyed then.

Ever since I finished medical school I make regular trips to Jamaica, sometimes several per year. On such visits I attend to my fellow countrymen as their physician. I give them free food, clothes, and other necessities. Recently I served the country on a contractual basis as a medical officer of health in a crucial time when typhoid fever was an epidemic. After four years, we were able to eradicate the causing factors.

On my first trip home shortly after graduation from college, a wealthy man who lived some three miles from my district invited me to stay at his home because he felt it was far more convenient than my mother's house. He tried to convince me that my mother would welcome the idea. I told him that going back home was a great excitement. It offered me the opportunity to go back to my birthplace, to retrace my childhood days, to meet old schoolmates, to visit my old stomping grounds, to remind me of what I was, to see changes that had taken place, to sleep on my old bed, to enjoy the fresh morning air while listening to the rooster crow and the birds whistle, to eat again from the family table. To me, that was fabulous and exciting, and the very thought was invigorating.

When was the last time you went home? If you haven't been home in a while, is it because of busyness or shame? For the young girl in the next story, it was an issue of shame, but she failed to think about her mother's feelings because she was consumed with her own.

Her mother had struggled for years as a single parent to keep her only daughter in college. She worked double shifts as a housekeeper and suffered many deprivations, to the extent that she could not afford to buy anything new to attend her daughter's graduation. She made certain her daughter had everything she needed to be well dressed and beautiful for her great day, but she had nothing new to wear. The young graduate was ashamed to see her mother arrived in a cheap dress and old and worn shoes. She appeared tired and old fashioned. Because her friends' parents were sophisticated and expensively dressed, she felt humiliated to introduce her mother and acted as if she did not know her. Her mother was not properly dressed for the occasion, so she was ignored as an unwanted stranger. She was too old to walk with the young and too poor to mix with the rich. She was the mother who chose to be poor and old fashioned to give her daughter the opportunity to be rich and popular. In disappointment and frustration, she took a taxi home. She had worked so hard and waited so long to see this day, only to be brushed aside because she didn't meet the standards of society.

So many of us have forsaken our parents because they are old fashioned. We are consumed with our jobs, our friends, or our careers, and we have no time for them. We ship them off to nursing homes because they are hard to please, they are miserable, or they are in the way. *It is easy to forget the ones who suffered sleepless nights to meet our needs.* They borrowed and sweated and suffered deprivations and shame to see us through. Wrinkles are on their faces because of worry and aging, and they may not be as stable in their thoughts, but these are the scars they bear for seeing you through. Is it too much to make a call, to drop a note, to send a card, to send some flowers, to make a surprise visit, to take them out to lunch, or even to embrace and express some words of cheer and love? It means so much just to hear you say, "Mom (or Dad), I love you." It is so easy to forget, avoid, and take things for granted. We can always get another job or find new friends, but parents cannot be replaced. It is the only commandment that has longevity attached to it: "Honor your father and your mother, that your days may be long upon the land which the Lord your God is giving you" (Exodus 20:12).

Sadly, not every child honors his or her parents. One young man abused his mother, cursed his father, and walked out on his own. Sixteen years went by without speaking to his parents. One night while on his way to the movies he passed by a tent and felt compelled to slow down because the singing reminded him of the music he used to enjoy at home when he was younger. As he neared the tent, the singing sounded sweeter and sweeter. He sat through the entire song service and was so inspired that he decided to stay for the sermon. He was spellbound and felt every word was meant for him. He was totally convicted and decided to go up with the others to give his heart to the Lord. He joined the church and was baptized. He was excited and wanted to go back home, but having been away so long and remembering how he had left, he did not know what to do. He consulted with the pastor, who told him to get in touch with his parents by letter and let them know he was now a baptized member of the church and wanted to come home. That night he wrote the following letter:

Dear Mom and Dad,

By the time you get this letter, I will be on the morning train on my way home. I have been baptized, and am now a member of the church. I am very sorry to have been such a terrible son.

I don't know if you really want me back home. If you do, kindly hang a white sheet on the clothesline. I am anxious to come home, so I will be looking for the sheet.

Your son,
Robert

Although the father got several letters that day, this one attracted his attention. He remembered the handwriting, and true enough, it was special. It was from a son who had not written for sixteen years. The message was incredible. He shouted to his wife, "Honey, you will not believe this. Our son is coming back home." His wife was overwhelmed with joy and burst into tears. "He wants us to hang a white sheet on the line as a sign that he is welcome home."

She shouted, "But, honey, I can't remember where the line was when he left. We have changed it so many times."

Her husband suggested, "Let us string a line all around the house, and let us hang all the white shirts, pajamas, towels, sheets, pillow slips, dresses, and towels on the line so that wherever he looks, he will see nothing but white clothes. Let us tell him by these white clothes that he is welcome back home."

Only parents could plan such a warm reception.

Going back home means a lot for parents who have been talking about you, thinking about you, and longing to see you. A call rejuvenates them, just to hear your voice. A letter invigorates them, just to know you are thinking about them. But a visit adds life and health, just to see you, feel you, and enjoy your embrace. When was the last time you visited your parents? Look back over your life. Has anyone helped you in some way or the other to make it through? It is so easy to forget. Some of us have made commitments and have failed to keep them. The trend is to overlook and take things for granted, yet it is important to thank the people who love you and have sacrificed for you.

Ten men had been isolated from home, from family, and from society. They were struck with the incurable disease known as leprosy. Their chances of being part of society again were too remote even to conceive. One day Jesus met them and gave them instructions as to where to go and what to do to be healed. On their way to the place they were sent, they discovered their leprosy was gone. They were clean. That was a moment of incredible excitement. All but one ran in diverse directions to reunite with wives and families to enjoy some of the good things and privileges they had been deprived of. However, one chose to forego the celebration and retrace his steps. Jesus was a busy man, and by then He could have been anywhere because He did not carry a preplanned itinerary. But this man found Jesus, the Man who had cured him. When he found Him, all he said was, "Thank you." Have you forgotten to say thank you to those who have supported you?

Going through medical school can be very challenging, especially with a growing family and limited funds. It is really a blessing to have a wife who unflinchingly stands by your side during those trying times. My wife did odd jobs in order to supplement our limited cash. She made immeasurable sacrifices. She worked, she prayed, she had sleepless nights filled with anxious moments. The wear and tear of medical school takes a toll on the ones closest to you. It is tempting to forget all those who helped you once you become successful. The following story illustrates this concept beautifully.

The chime of the old town clock was the clarion call that kept everyone who heard it going to work on time. One morning everyone was late for work because the old clock stopped chiming. After numerous attempts to fix it, a guard was placed at the tower in order to preserve the clock because so many repairmen had tried in vain to fix it. One morning after several months had passed an old beggar dressed in rags and carrying an old bundle passed by and noticed the clock was not working. Looking up, he sought permission to fix it but was ordered to move on. When the guard was distracted, the beggar snuck up the tower and, in few minutes, with his bare hands, repaired the old clock. The chime was once again heard throughout the city.

The excitement over hearing the chime again was so great that officers, secretaries, and government officials rushed out to the tower to celebrate and compliment the expert who had fixed the clock and brought life back to the city. To their amazement, it was an old beggar in rags with a dirty bundle who had done the job. When questioned, he explained that it was easy because he had built the clock with his own hands thirty years before.

However bright the present may be, you should not allow it to becloud the red seas nor the dark wilderness through which you traveled to be where you are. It has often been said that adversity keeps one on their knees.

A classmate and roommate of mine had been a devout church member all his college days. After receiving his doctorate, he began to climb the ladder of success. Soon he was numbered among the wealthy. He completely lost interest in religion and considered church an unnecessary ritual. To him, life was at its best when one was in a position to get whatever one needed without having to beg or borrow. He indicated that recreational outlets such as the golf course, the clubhouse, and the movies were far more rewarding than church. *It is very unfortunate when one allows the blessings to turn one's back on the source of the blessings.*

Cecelia Jones was a young lady in her early twenties when she rebelled against the discipline of home and decided to leave. She got a job and lived in a nearby city with friends. Several months went by, and late one night, she decided to go for a ride. She chose to take the road that passed her mother's house. As she approached the gate, she slowed down, and as she looked at the house, she had flashbacks to old childhood days. She eventually parked the car so she could get a good view of her room. She looked closely and noticed the door to her mother's room was wide open. She was surprised because she remembered her mother had always kept her door closed during the night. She began to think that an intruder had entered her room and probably hurt her. Rushing to the room, she found that her mother was quite safe and resting peacefully. As she turned to leave, she heard her mother's voice. "Cecelia, is that you?"

She ran and hugged her, and with tears in her eyes, she said, "Oh Mother, why did you forget to close your door?"

Joyfully, her mother replied, "Honey, ever since you left, that door has always been left open for you to come back home."

Similarly, the door to the church and to God is always open. If you have distanced yourself from God and not properly thanked Him for His steadfast kindness, then by all means come home to His body of believers.

Ingratitude can be described as distasteful in that it is the basic cause of most mental agony and regrets encountered in life. The ungrateful person becomes a specialist in finding faults, in identifying mistakes, and being judgmental. Such people are specialists in magnifying mistakes and downplaying the good. They refuse to look in the mirror because they consider themselves perfect. They are suspicious, insecure, jealous, and evil.

I once read a ten-page letter written by an angry husband, every line packed with reasons why he was divorcing his wife of sixteen years. It was a full summary of faults he had been bottling up from the early years of their courtship. One of his complaints was that her cooking was distasteful and non-nutritious. *Love covers a multitude of faults, and those that are not covered are not magnified.* He could have presented her a surprise gift of a cookbook or helped with the grocery and menu planning. Or he could have done some of the cooking or even sent her to a cooking school if her cooking was honestly that bad. He could have spent some time with her in the kitchen. If he was not a good cook, he could have helped in cutting up the vegetables, making the salad, preparing the dessert, or washing the dishes.

During my sixty years of marriage, I have maintained a taste for my wife's cooking. I look forward to being with the family at the dining table. Because her meals are always so enjoyable, I refuse to eat out, however tempting it might be. I cook sometimes and help her with the dishes, shopping, and menu planning.

Working together adds taste and sweetness to life. Quite often, my wife would ask, "Honey, what would you like for dinner today?" Then she would list the options. I never forget to thank her and compliment her for her cooking. It helps her know I appreciate what she is doing. She is not my maid. We are lovers.

According to that angry husband's letter, his wife spent too much time on the phone. This, of course, can be dangerous if it leads to rumors, gossiping, or involvement in family disputes. Husbands who have little or no time to spend with their wives may feel lonely. Our jobs can rob us of our home life. Social engagements should include wives so that they do not become bored and isolated. Housework can be taxing and tiresome, just as much as a full-time job outside the home. If the wife works at a full-time job, then her burden is even greater; however, it is important to carve out sufficient time to spend together. If, as was the case with this gentleman, his wife spent time on the phone when he was home, then he might have explored the possibility that there was a communication gap between them.

Some men are poor talkers, but you can play games together, watch a good movie, or just go walking together when the weather is nice. Lovers shouldn't be critical of each other. If it becomes necessary to monitor every telephone call or go around peeping and scrutinizing every action, it's time to go back to courting days and repeat some of the little things you were accustomed to doing to protect and ensure love was in action. It is not the big things, the expensive gifts, or the fanciful, but little tokens of love. A hidden candy in a pocket says a lot when given as a surprise. A little gift that is expressive reveals deep emotions that go further than words.

As I read the pages of that derogatory letter, I saw a man who hoped he would be the last man in that woman's life, as he expected any man who read the letter would have reason to stay far away from her because she was no good. We should spend more time looking for the good and dig a grave to bury the encountered evil.

As an example, two prisoners were caught looking through the bars in the same direction. Looking down at the nearest lake, one saw the heavy mud from the trampling feet of thirsty cows. To him, it was obnoxious and distasteful. The other prisoner saw the beautiful white lilies blooming in their splendor and spreading their sweet aroma to conceal the mud's stench and ugliness.

A man who has made his share of mistakes is a specialist in identifying faults in other people. He generally sees what he is looking for. At the root of criticism and faultfinding is ingratitude. It is so easy to forget the days of courtship when all was golden and sweet. The sky was always blue, and the comb was always full of honey. Even the most expensive painting carries an ugly side. Anyone who spends his time looking at it will never enjoy the beauty, the elegance, and the irresistible thrill of the other side. Let us spend more time searching and enjoying the pleasures of life that the ugly often overshadows. In a world where everything is traded in for the latest model, I encourage you to overcome these trends by remembering the support system that got you to where you are.

Chapter 10
You Are a Survivor

Did you know that you were born to survive? Look in the mirror. The person who is looking at you is a born survivor. Smile, and your reflection smiles back at you. You are indeed a reflection of your mind. The world sees in you what your mind is telling you. If you are happy in your mind, the world has reason to know you are at peace with yourself because you will be singing or smiling. On the other hand, if you are worried, frustrated, anxious, disturbed, or disappointed, then the onlooker will see a sad or sick person. He will have reason to ask if everything is all right with you. We should not go around advertising our problems on our faces.

Monday morning conversations in the elevator often focus on the negative. People seem so disgruntled about everything. They seem so tired. "The weekend went by so fast. Boy, I wish this were Friday. I am just tired. I need some more rest." "This job is getting on my nerves. I need a new job." "Boy, I just hate Mondays." They seem to be tired of life and always anxious to be somewhere else. People stare at me when, in response to their question, "How are you?" I say, "Fine, I have no reason to complain." It is always good to remind yourself that however bad things are for you, there are others who are ten times worse. The story is told of a young man who kept putting off going to church because he needed a new pair of shoes. He was tired of wearing the same pair every week. Then one day he ran into a young man who had no feet but was on his way to church.

You need to have faith in yourself. Columbus encountered many frustrations on his first voyage. His men threatened a mutiny because the wide ocean did nothing to quiet there doubt. Columbus was confident that his goal was achievable. He believed the world was round, and he was determined to prove it. Despite the threats and unpredictable nature of the ocean, he kept moving on because he had faith. *Regardless of what others think or how they feel, the thing that matters is what you think about yourself and your determination to achieve your goal.* Those who have tried and failed will always preach failure. Those who failed because the way was obscured by a lack of funds, lack of support, or other difficulties will be bad companions or advisors. The world is searching for individuals who are strong enough to defend their convictions though they are derided, criticized, or deserted. You need to convince yourself that you are such a person.

The power of persuasion is a convincing element in the decision making process. Your greatest enhancement of success is a mind fully persuaded to succeed, come what may. There is greater satisfaction in having achieved despite pitfalls than to have lost because you failed to try. To have tried and failed is no disgrace. The dilemma lies in how long you stay in your failure. Failures are intended to be steppingstones. Some of the world's greatest achievements are the results of many failures. The secret lies in finding what contributed to the failure and setting up strategies to avoid repeating them. The light bulb came after some ninety-nine failures, but every time Edison failed he would add that which he had failed to have added, thus correcting that which was done wrong. You should have the courage to face the odds. Odds can be made into barriers or converted into steppingstones. You determine what role barriers play in your life.

At fifteen I was threatened and condemned by a devil worshiper. I was destined to be a permanent failure, according to him. To many, his prediction was infallible, but to me it was a challenge. I studied twice as hard and eliminated failure completely from my mind. I thought, lived, and acted positively. I had a goal, and I could not afford to have anyone, whether saint or devil, dissuade me from achieving it. I did make it.

At age twenty I was branded stupid and too primitive to make it by one of my college professors. To other students this was prophetic, but to me it was a challenge. I put my conviction to the test, and with God's help, I survived her judgment and was shortly afterward complimented by her as her favorite and most reliable student.

At age twenty-three one of my theology coordinators predicted I was not destined to be a good preacher. I wondered what his standard of judgment was, but I did not take his prediction as a reason to change my course. However, he succeeded in frustrating my other classmates who, on his advice, changed their ambition. I took it as a challenge. I have been a very successful pastor and a renowned international preacher.

At age thirty my employer advised me that I was too old to go to medical school. I was too established in my ministry. I had a young family of four children, and from a social point of view, I had made my name. He reminded me of the unpredictable nature of years of study, the cost, and the sacrifices, which would create undue stress on the family. He was sincere in his judgment, because I was one of his favorite and most productive workers. He hoped to change my mind, and I appreciated his fatherly concern, but I had to decide on my own. Should I consider my advanced age as a barrier to further educational goals? Should I be scared to face the unpredictable, whether it is hard work, financial burden, or undue stress? I was fully prepared to take the challenge, and I did. I entered medical school, and despite the difficulties and stress, I graduated as a full-fledged physician.

During my first year as a premed student, I was fired from my job, had a foreclosure notice on my car, and was the victim of a dangerous tornado. Were the odds telling me to quit? Each event seemed to ask me, are you still determined to be a physician? My answer was "yes." I could not afford to forget how divine intervention had always helped me survive. Thus, I was reassured more and more and became more determined to press on toward reaching my goal. I felt that I was being tested on the strength of my determination to achieve my goal. God could have been using these experiences to keep me trusting in Him because each time I faced these odds, I found myself clinging closer to and holding more firmly to His promises.

Two weeks before I entered medical school, an experienced physician strongly advised me to take up nursing instead of medicine. The stakes were stacked against me. The list was a long one. The costs were escalating each year. Grades were highly competitive, and I would be facing a group of students who had youth in their favor. The time period was long and tedious. The list of sacrifices was stupendous. The chances of not making it became greater. Thus far, I had received no encouragement from anyone, but I had what it took to face all of the naysayers. I had set my face as a flint, and I was determined to reach my goal.

> **Knowing yourself is an indispensable ingredient for reaching your goals.**

Six weeks after starting class, I discovered I was actually repeating premed. I had enrolled in the wrong program because of my limited Spanish. I thought I was sitting in the right class. Thus, I lost my first semester of medical school. Was this a sign that I should quit? No, it was another challenge. I turned it into a steppingstone. My family and I went back home and spent the time earning some money. *If you and I could see as far as God sees, we would choose to be led just the way God leads, and so it is justifiable to say all things work for good to them that love God.* Some obstacles force us to worry, but we should not allow them to become stumbling blocks.

And then, as you remember, I almost lost my chance to finish medical school because I thought I got an F on my final human physiology exam. Fortunately, with the help of a classmate who had seen my actual grade, I appealed the case and discovered that someone out of spite had deliberately changed my grade. Had I not succeeded in having it changed I would no doubt be numbered among the many other victims who had to drop out of medical school. I could have chosen to be like the other students who felt it was futile to fight against the odds. They chose to take the path of least resistance.

Knowing yourself is an indispensable ingredient for reaching your goals. You have to be true to your convictions as the compass needle is to the pole. Success is failure turned inside out. The silver tint of the clouds of doubt may conceal the brilliance of the stars beyond, so you can never know how close you are. It may be near when it seems so far. You need to stick to the fight when you are hardest hit. It's when things seem worse that you can't afford to quit. Keep reminding yourself you have what it takes to face the odds. You ought to have what it takes to know the difference between the positive and the negative. A devoted friend, a trusted boss, or a supervisor may give you advice that sounds or appears sincere, but what if they focus on the unpredictable hardships and difficulties as reason for not pursuing your goal? Your aim in such instances should be to think of the possible odds as the negative side and try to see the positive side. One can either succeed or fail, and in pursuit of success, be prepared to see the unpredictable difficulties and hardships as the counterpart to success. Should you try to separate or avoid them, success will not be fully appreciated. So, endeavor to see the negatives as the other side of success. Should someone who has experienced failure after several attempts to succeed try to dissuade you from pursuing your goal, remember that his failure may be due to his doing the right thing the wrong way. Instead, try to reverse failure by doing the right thing the right way. By failing to prepare, you are preparing to fail.

> **Dealing with a problem without finding its cause is focusing on the negative.**

Dealing with a problem without finding its cause is focusing on the negative, which is exactly what one supervisor did when he submitted a list of unexplained absences as a justifiable reason for recommending one of his employees for dismissal or disciplinary action. On reviewing his file, I discovered that this employee's record proved him to be very diligent and productive. There upon

I decided to do a field visit and personally talk with the employee in question. Upon reviewing his time chart, I learned that the absences were routinely on the same day of every month. His record otherwise was superb. On questioning him about these absences, he explained that those were the days when his itinerary took him in the opposite direction from the office. He saved taxi fare by not duplicating his trip, which was approximately twenty miles one way.

Unless we look for answers and focus on the positive, one will never see the other side of the problem. In his attempt to dissuade me from entering medicine, my employer presented me with a long list of others who had tried and failed. However, he failed to show me the long list of those who had succeeded and are doing well. A practicing physician tried to discourage me from going into medicine by recounting the difficulties, the heavy costs, the long hours of studying, the years of internship, and all the other innumerable problems he encountered in medical school, but he forgot to mention the satisfaction he was enjoying as a successful physician.

The highway to success is crowded with positives and negatives. A person who has had a taste of a sour lemon appreciates the taste of something sweet. Likewise, one who has been in the dark room appreciates even a spark of light. Negatives enhance the appreciation for positives. Therefore, accustom yourself to think and act positively, and the negatives will become steppingstones.

One negative that I faced toward the end of medical school was the fact that I was forced to take some summer classes to meet the requirements for graduation. This compromised my usual summer schedule of going back home to make money to meet the budget for the next six months of school. My wife volunteered to work while I went to summer school. But her salary was very minimal, so I had to think of other resources for meeting the registration deadline for my last semester. I kept hoping a miracle would show up. Each day, as the mailman passed by, I hoped for a letter bringing me a check from the bank of heaven. This never happened. I visited the post office every day with the thought that no doubt a letter would come. With every envelope marked with an airmail stamp, I hoped it was mine. The last day for registration came, but the long hoped for check had not arrived.

Mark you, I had no guarantee from anyone; therefore, my not receiving a check was earmarked with anxiety rather than frustration. I had prayed earnestly about it and had strong confidence in God. In a situation like this, the negatives had become the prevailing factor. All the chances of my receiving a miracle check by mail had turned out to be just fantasies. They seemed to be saying, "Well, no money, no registration, no classes. So what's next? Why not quit?"

On the other side of the coin, the positive instinct was saying, "Don't quit, don't give up; there is still a chance. God has some other recourse. Keep on trusting." What could I do next? That was my last day to register, which also meant my chances of being numbered among the graduates were at great risk. A small voice said to me, "Have you exhausted all the options? Do you really want to be a physician?" Surely I had made up my mind that despite the fact I did not have any money, I was not going to let the last chance pass by without being registered.

I got up, got dressed, assembled my documents, and started out like a millionaire for the registration line. On reaching the office, I joined a long line of students who, like me, were making use of the last chance. Some of them were also there to register for the last time. I found myself standing in a line that was getting closer and closer to the window of reckoning. I had all my documents, but I had no money. It all seemed like a dream, but it was real. I had no plan and no idea of what would be the outcome. I was there in line still hoping for a miracle. I believed that it was far too late for God to say no after He had said yes so many times. I kept thinking back to the many crisis moments I had endured since I began pursuing my goal to be a physician and how much convincing evidence I had that God was with me. It was very difficult to conceive of any way a miracle could be brought at such a critical time. Never the less, my hope was strong, and all I was doing was proving to God that I expected Him to work it out in some way.

The line inched closer and closer to the window. When I was the tenth person in line, a fellow student joined the end and shouted, "Williams, how come you are just registering? I thought I was the only late person to register."

I replied with a smile, "I have been waiting on you to get the funds to register."

> God delights in extreme situations where no one can question divine intervention.

The comment was intended to be a joke, but all of a sudden, he said, "Were you really waiting for me?"

I assured him it was only a joke. He insisted, "Williams, I have a funny feeling it was not a joke. Something is telling me you really need some money. Here is a blank check, take it and use it as you wish. You have been a good friend; you owe me nothing."

I asked him why he was doing that. I assured him I was not asking him to do so. He replied, "You have done me a lot of good; this is my way of saying thank you. I have been waiting for a long time for this chance to show you my appreciation. Please don't refuse it."

In a few minutes, I was fully registered for my last semester. My mustard seed faith had moved the mountain. It proved that *God has a thousand and one ways of showing His interest in our well being and in answering our prayers.*

When we pray to Him in simple faith and believe that He will provide, He opens the floodgates of heaven for His children (see Psalm 103:13).

There is a story in the Bible that tells about a widow who was collecting wood in order to make her son and her last meal (see 1 Kings 17). After she used the last flour in the barrel, there would be no other resources from which they could buy, borrow, or beg from because there was a famine in the land. You may wonder why Elijah did not show up a week or even a day before, but God sent him when they had come to the last drop in the barrel, and so it was the last day. God delights in extreme situations where no one can question divine intervention. When the woman had come to the last day with the last drop, God took over, and her last became the beginning of many, many more days with enough to last the entire famine. "Yea, though I walk through the valley of the shadow of death, I will fear no evil; for You are with me; Your rod and Your staff, they comfort me" (Psalm 23:4).

Every night, however dark or long it may be, is always followed by day, and every storm, however raging it might be, is always followed by calm. In your struggle to achieve your goal, you will encounter dark nights and dangerous storms, but keep pressing on because the darkest part of the night is always the moment before dawn. *Negatives will always appear whenever you are searching for positives.* If one is not careful, the predominance of negatives will lead to frustration, which, when misinterpreted, will force one to give up. There are scores of capable people who are living up to less than half of their potential. They have succumbed to the haunting spell of negatives, which aggressively exploit the anxious, the unstable, and the bewildered. *Survival is determined by the height and depth of your desire to succeed.* Probabilities will build up strong expectations, but when they run out, realities can only be authenticated by your determination to succeed despite multiple pitfalls.

You need to convince yourself you have what it takes to make it. Sometime ago I was on my way to visit an old friend whom I had not seen for ages. I had a fairly good idea where he lived, but not having been there for such a long time and with so many changes in the streets and houses, I found it very difficult to find my way. I stopped and asked an elderly man about my friend and the way to his home. He gave me the impression he knew the person and the way to his house. His directions, however, were somewhat misleading, and I found myself going in the opposite direction. The person he knew must have been someone else. There were certain landmarks that stood out in my mind, so although there were notable changes in the environment, there were some significant marks or signs that remained unchanged. I, therefore, chose to follow my instinct and eventually found my friend's house despite some difficulties. Some folks are just so willing to help that, despite the fact that they can't, they will still try because they don't want to say no.

The choice of being a doctor, a nurse, a mechanic, or a horticulturist is solely yours. You have to follow the landmarks of your own life goals and pursue them at all costs. You cannot rely on someone else to tell you what to do. If you are totally convinced that such a choice is the right one, then you need to convince yourself that you have what it takes to reach your goal. A friend told me he wanted to be a lawyer because there is a lot of money in that field. A fellow classmate admitted he wanted to be a physician because of the prestige and the high pay. Motives form the basis for making decisions, and they do differ for every person.

Ever since my elementary school days, I wanted to be a physician. When I visited the library, I checked out health-related books. When I entered college, I was motivated to be a medical missionary, so I took up theology. I love preaching and really enjoy pastoral engagements. But in all my pastoral years, I had not given up my desire to be a physician, and so it was quite difficult to be dissuaded because I was fully motivated.

I was aware of the odds and was prepared to accept the challenges. I had enough experiences to be convinced that I had what it took to make it. I definitely knew I did not have the funds, but I realized I had the prerequisites that qualified me to get the funds. Once you are certain you have chosen the right career, you need to make a thorough assessment to be totally convinced you really have what it takes to reach your goal. *Your motive will certainly influence your achievement.* Why have you chosen your career? Is it because a family member has been very successful in that field? That is an asset in your favor. You have the advantage of doing some orientation with them, or you can discuss with them in detail the pros and the cons of entering that field. They can suggest strategies to pass by some of the roadblocks so that the unavoidable does not catch you unaware.

Your choice may be made on just personal inclinations. Do some research on the subject. Be selective in your study courses. Talk with folks who are experienced. Be aware of the mountains you will have to climb, and don't let friends or foes frighten you about them. Once you are cognizant of the hills and valleys, make up your mind to meet them. It can be very frightening if you enter the journey blindly. Be prepared and boldly face the challenges. Remember, you have convinced yourself you have what it takes to make it. So don't allow anyone to turn you around.

> **People are more prone to help you inish than they are to help you start.**

Your next question may be, "How am I going to make it?" This is a justifiable question because the realities must be faced and overcome. In every journey the most important achievement is covering the first mile because you will be one mile nearer to your destination. If you stop to worry about the miles ahead, you will never start. Whatever the first mile may be, aim at finishing it. It may be an application, a telephone call, an appointment, or a visit for an interview. Don't wait in fear of the unknown. Learn to live one day at a time. Do not wait to get all the funds before you start. People are more prone to help you finish than they are to help you start. I am inclined to pick up a hitchhiker who is walking than one who is standing waiting to be picked up. If you plan to pray for rain, make certain you stop the leaks in the roof and the gutters, and that catchments are in good shape before you pray. That is faith in action. If you are hoping your application will be favorably considered, make certain all the other prerequisites are in order.

I exhibited my faith in action one time when my three sons were in medical school some 1,800 miles away. One night just around bedtime, I got a call from them saying it was imperative for me to come right away to clear up some problems in their registration process. Without hesitation I promised to be there. I then presented the problems to the Lord and gave Him thanks for solving them for me. The next morning I started out very early to drive the 1,800 miles. Two hundred miles away from home, something dawned on me. I recalled having asked God to solve the problems for me and had given Him thanks for doing so. As I had done so and had confirmed my confidence that He would solve them by saying thank you, why was I making this long journey? Was I contradicting my own faith in God? I then prayed and asked God to forgive me for my lack of faith. I cancelled my plans and turned back.

On reaching home I got another call from my boys. This time the message was, "Daddy, we are so glad we caught you before you left. Please don't worry about coming. The dean, recognizing us as your sons, has cleared the way and given us permission to register." If God is your Father and He is leading you, why should you be concerned about how you are going to make it? Since He knows the way, you will do yourself a great favor in just allowing Him to lead while you follow. He has promised that, just as a father, He will answer when His child calls (see Luke 15:11–26). He has opened many closed doors for me, and however, closed yours might be, He is more than able to open it. Since you know where you are going, just keep on until you arrive.

It takes a lot of courage and faith to pursue something without knowing how you are going to make it. At the Red Sea, there were no boats or ferries, and Pharaoh and his army were fast approaching. The question from a nervous, fearful crowd was, "How are we going to make it?" The answer was, "Stand still, and see the salvation of the Lord" (Exodus 14:13). *It takes a lot of faith to stand still in moments like these, but God delights in showing His power when man faces extremes.* Moses' rod, through the power of God, when stretched across the roaring Red Sea, pushed back the water and turned it into dry ground. You may not have a rod, but you have faith in a living God who is stronger than anyone or anything. We can trust and believe in Him because He said, "I will be with you."

I had just bought my first car and succeeded in getting my driver's license. My wife thought it would be exciting to take our baby boy, who was only four months old at the time, to see her parents in our new car. This was only a ninety-minute drive away. My greatest problem in driving then was changing the gears. Sometimes I waited too late to downshift gears so I often would stall the car, especially on the hills. As we set out on our trip, we encountered rain. Using the lights and wipers, and frequently stalling the car resulted in the battery dying.

We succeeded in getting a boost in a nearby city, but it was not enough to carry us far, and we ended up stalled on a dense, swampy road some three miles away from her parents. It was pitch dark, and the mosquitoes were plentiful. Although she was very scared, my wife felt that I should walk back to the city to seek some help since no cars were passing our way. I blatantly refused because I felt it was unsafe to leave them in the dark and in such isolation. I assured her God would send someone to help us soon.

Within a few minutes, a car drove up. On stopping the driver and telling him our problem he shook his head and remarked that we must have been praying because under ordinary circumstances he would not have stopped for anything in an area like that. He said he was going to do something he had never done for anyone before. He opened his car trunk, took out a generator, and charged my battery for free. In a few minutes, we were on our way, rejoicing in God's protection and providence.

We did not know who this man was, but one thing was evident: we had no reason to fear any evil because God's angels were surrounding us (see Psalm 34:7). We all, at some time or another, will come across occasions when we are forced to wonder how we are going to make it, but the Bible is loaded with a multitude of moments when God opened ways and provided means in times of desperate need. Jesus repeatedly said, in so many words, "Take no thought about what you will eat or drink because your heavenly Father has enough for all those who trust in Him" (see Matthew 6:30–32).

A young man, upon hearing the experiences I had in pursuing medicine, gave up his job, left his family of four, and started premedical studies. Within six months, he began to face the realities of classwork. His wife became upset and wanted him to come home. His savings ran out, and financial stress crept in. He began to realize that dreams can camouflage emotion. He gave up and went back home. This represents a true picture of many who begin the race but, when pressed by prevailing circumstances, chose to change course and join the list of those who tried and failed.

Shortly after I started premedical studies, I began to find it very difficult to meet some of my monthly bills. I appealed to my brother for help because he was financially stable. He agreed to take care of some of my bills. But on his way home he called to tell me he had changed his mind. He then advised me to give up the idea of being a physician and go back to preaching. I told him thanks for his advice, but instead of giving up as he suggested, I revised my program to meet the demand. The university I was attending was 200 miles from home, which impeded my ability to work because I was forced to stay on campus. I switched to a university closer to home and got a full-time night job.

There is always a way around a barrier. I always felt that if one succeeds in parking, he should find it easier to get out of his parking spot. It is so easy to give up. I was fully aware that faith with works is rewarding, and I endeavored to exercise faith in myself. I had become a specialist in differentiating the negatives from the positives, and I embraced the fact that within me there was a dominant desire to survive. With such a background, I deliberately chose to achieve my goal. To reach your goal, you have to be focused. You can't afford to hang onto faith alone. You need to set your goal and then strategize ways of reaching it. Then make up your mind to reach it come what may. This, in a nutshell, is how you build self-confidence. *If you believe you can do it, then prove it to yourself by doing it.* Choices generally come with options. Your expectations or aspirations should not be influenced by emotions or by what you see or hear.

Emotionally you can be misguided, and your thinking can become irrational. Generally, what you see in others who have achieved may be misleading, for their methodology, circumstances, and motives may be different from yours. What you hear may be derogatory or complimentary. You should be influenced by an instinct that generates a strong will to achieve your goal regardless of the circumstances.

Ten men were sent out to view the land of Canaan. Moses wanted some firsthand information about this new country. He was interested in knowing about the people, their strength, the land, its productivity, and the type of buildings he would encounter in his attempt to capture the land. He had no reference or history books or any other resources to give him any type of information. He was assigned to capture this land and establish cities for the millions of people he was leading. How these men interpreted what they saw or heard would set the pace for the campaign ahead. Eight men saw the giant sons of Anak and

> **You should be influenced by an instinct that generates a strong will to achieve your goal regardless of the circumstances.**

felt the Israelites were like grasshoppers in comparison. They were too strong and were loaded with gallantry and ammunitions far superior to the weapons the host of Israel possessed. The walls were impregnable, so tall and wide that the puny army of Israel could not surmount them. In other words, it was too ambitious even to try to invade. Well after they had crossed the Red Sea, they were now in the heart of a strange land and were being told they needed to turn back because the obstacles were too great. Does this sound familiar?

The other two men saw things differently. They saw fertility. The grapes were fabulous. The terrain was fantastic and was potentially filled with milk and honey. They did not see giants; they saw victory. They did not see great walls that were impregnable. They had confidence and faith in the God who had divided the Red Sea and destroyed Pharaoh and his army. They believed that He was more than able to give them victory over the giants with all their gallantry. Caleb and Joshua saw lilies where the others saw nothing but mud. They saw opportunities where the others saw defeat and failure (see Psalm 27:14). It is a fact that one sees what he looks for and hears what supports his thinking. If you are going to make it, you will have to have the eyes and ears of Joshua and Caleb. You will have to start looking for what enhances your vision and your dream. Like Caleb and Joshua, you need to see difficulties as steppingstones and problems as challenges. *Reaching your goal is a matter of choice and is achievable if you choose to make it.*

Chapter 11
Surviving Directions

In what direction are you heading? Are you headed north, south, east, or west? Each direction carries you toward fulfilling your destiny. One's choice is based on your goals.

Northbound

Generally, the northbound route is the way up. People always say, "We are going up North." Whenever one attempts to go "up," there is always the associated thought of energy output and strong willpower. Some people who face physical adversities such as arthritis, respiratory, or cardiovascular diseases are hesitant to make the northbound trip. Such people are obsessed with fear and refuse to see things positively. Time, cost, and sacrifice appear as roadblocks. This route takes more time because it is generally longer, and the rate of speed is slower, thus it is also more costly.

All good careers are highly competitive, and admission to institutions that prepare for such fields are very selective. The benefits are fabulous, and the life is superb, but it takes more time, it costs a lot, the sacrifices are great, and the chances for failure are high. However, if one chooses to build in a hurry by using cheap materials, stability is compromised and early and frequent repairs will be faced. There is a tendency to choose the easy way out because one is in a hurry to make money. If one chooses to be a carpenter, the option of being just a person using a hammer to drive a nail and a saw to cut wood is theirs. They will only earn minimum wage. They can choose to spend some time learning to be a custom builder and enjoy the thrill of being a wanted carpenter, getting top rate pay for service. Whatever your ambition, strive to be the best. The demand for first-class service is very high—people are in search of quality service and are willing to pay for it.

I was flying from San Francisco to Atlanta and sat by a passenger who spent the entire flight talking about himself. He was a traveling salesman who took numerous trips to various places and enjoyed a bountiful list of fringe benefits. His itinerary was extensive, and his estates and achievements were fabulous. He gave me no chance to say anything about myself and did not even attempt to find out who I was or what I did. When he eventually ran out of words, I handed him my business card. On receiving it he became spellbound and in amazement shouted, "I can't believe it, do you mean that all this time I have been describing myself as the big accomplished guy, not knowing I was talking to a medical doctor with a PhD, an MPH, and a BTH? I really thought I was great, but you are ten times greater."

I was shocked to hear his words and told him he should never allow himself to be overtaken by an inferiority complex. Greatness is not measured by degrees but by the mind because the mind is the measure of the man. He should continue to feel great because he was excelling in what he enjoyed doing.

The word complex can be harmful if applied in the wrong context. If your achievements make you feel superior to others, you may show your feelings through selfishness. On the other hand, if you are encumbered with feelings of inferiority, you may be tempted to serve your boss as a slave with feelings of subordination. *Achievement should give us the justification to provide a service of the highest quality.* Whether you are a plumber, a gardener, or a physician, the service provided will meet the need that warrants it regardless of who receives it.

You may have already achieved your projected goal in life. What is your next move? Whatever your present status, you should aim to be at your best at all times. You may have been the boss's secretary for years. Are you at the same level you were when you first got the job? Have you become complacently satisfied in being just what you are? If you are heading northbound, then you should be changing gears to compete with the rising demands. You can't afford to be stalled on the hill. Strive to reach higher ground so that when opportunity knocks you will be considered qualified for promotion. Your boss may hate to lose you because of your efficiency, but you should give him or her reason to feel pricked by a guilty conscience should he or she refrain from recommending you for something higher. You should give yourself a chance to take some classes at night or an online course to make yourself available for something higher when the opportunity arises. Don't be satisfied until you have reached the top of your potential. Aim at being a worker in demand.

Years after I finished medical training, I saw the opportunity to be an epidemiologist. I sacrificed the time to prepare myself for the challenge. I took the time off, and with the incentive of a scholarship, I acquired a master's degree in public health. This widened my perspective, and I enjoyed the opportunities it gave me to provide qualified services. Being on the northbound route, I saw areas yet unreached in my field, and so I reached to cover such areas and acquired a doctorate in holistic medicine. This gave me the opportunity to meet the current demand for such expertise. One should never be complacently satisfied. At the end of the northbound journey, there will be, above all things, the satisfaction of achievement.

A wealthy man advertised for a competent chauffeur. The road to his home was steep, winding, and dangerous. Three men responded to the advertisement. During the interview, the first applicant boasted of his dexterity and years of driving. He claimed that at sixty miles per hour he could make those winding roads without the least fear of having an accident. The second applicant promised to travel with only one finger on the steering wheel at any speed and make it home safely. His daily travel took him over winding and precipitous highways so he guaranteed safe driving. The third applicant expressed concern about the winding roads and the dangerous precipice and promised that with such concerns and the well being of all in mind, he would be as careful as possible in his driving in order to avoid all hazards. He got the job. *It is not how long you have been doing the job, what matters is how well you can do it.* If you plan to take the northern route, make up your mind to do it well.

Southbound

The southern route is generally considered the way down. In talking about the South, people generally say "down South." Going down is much easier than going up. In the Bible the southern route always describes a path that appears bright but generally ends with remorse. Lot, Abraham's nephew, chose Sodom because the grass was green and the potential appeared great. Eventually he regretted having taken the southern route and had to go north and start all over again. The prodigal son took his entire heritage and ventured south where he became very popular, but after squandering all his funds having a good time, he ended up with bitter remorse and regrets. He came to himself and took the northern route, which led back home, where he was joyfully welcomed by a forgiving father and given a land of new beginnings (see Luke 15:11–32). The southern route is always the easier way.

One of the greatest problems I had in my early days of driving was changing the gears on my stick shift car. I was somewhat slow in manipulating the clutch, so I ended up grinding the gears. It was a nerve-racking experience hearing the sound of the grinding gears, especially when you have roadside listeners. Thus, I would stay in a high gear too long, which caused the car to struggle and stall.

That's how fear works. It forces one to take the path of least resistance and keep gliding in high gear. This person becomes complacently satisfied with nothing. I overheard a young man exultantly saying to his friends, "I would rather remain as I am, although I am living off nothing, because I could not stand being laughed at if I were to try and fail. I'd feel like I was making a fool of myself. People might think I am too ambitious. They might think I don't know my own mind."

When I was a boy, I always wanted to learn to swim, but I was too scared to try. I admired how my friends could dive, float, and manipulate themselves in the water. I wished I could, but I was afraid. My best friend offered to teach me. He had me climb on his back and securely hold on to him. He then dove into the water. I got scared and let go of him. He apologized and promised he would not dive with me again. A short time after his pleading, I ventured out with him again. As soon as he started off, he dove with me again. I again let go and swore I would never trust him again. He again apologized and coaxed me into giving him just one more chance. He appeared so sincere that I agreed and chose to go with him again. As soon as he started, he again dove with me. But this time, I was not as scared as before. I was becoming used to diving. This time I did not let go, and when he emerged, I begged him to do it again. He did it twice, and by the third time, I began to kick my legs, and then my hands were free. That was the beginning of my first swimming lesson. By the end of the day, I was a swimmer because I overcame my fear. The downward stream will take you where it is going, but if you fight against it, you will eventually find yourself where you want to go.

People traveling the southbound route are, like Lot, anxious to get going, and they want it the easy way. Lot, on seeing the green grass, the fertile plains, and the potential for quick money, chose the south. Shortcuts can be dangerous. While in medical school, a student offered to sell me answers to the final exams. I refused his offer by telling him that cheating does not make good doctors. One does not buy his way into a career; he prepares and works for it.

The southbound route makes one vulnerable to evil tendencies. He is prone to take shortcuts, to deceive and to cover up. A contractor who had worked with the city council for more than thirty years had reached his retirement. His last contract was to build a four-bedroom house on a lot overlooking the city. As usual, he got an open order providing funds to purchase all of the materials. Realizing this was his last contract, he secretly hid all the good materials to build a house for himself and built the contractual house with cheap, low-grade materials. He did a good job covering up the defective materials with plaster and paint. On completion, he signed a written statement saying he had done a perfect job.

To his surprise, after he had taken the mayor for a walk through the home, he was handed the keys as a token of appreciation for his years of invaluable service to the council. Surprised and grateful as he was, he suppressed a deep feeling of remorse because he alone knew he had cheated himself and not the city. Soon he had to try to undo what he had done. The leaks, the cracks, and the other problems soon began to show. With regret, he tried to remedy the deception of his own hands.

The southbound route means the easy way. The prodigal son chose to live off his father's legacy. He got it at no cost, so losing it was easy. He had no budgetary restraints or projections, and that fostered carelessness and irresponsibility. The final stage was disaster. It proves anything one gets for nothing may to some extent value nothing.

We all need to have some reserve from which we can draw in times of need. *One's richest reserve is his pool of experiences acquired in his struggle to survive.* I recall days when I walked the busy streets knocking on business doors in search of a job. Those were days when I had no money and no food. All I had to survive was a piece of sugar cane. I cut it in small pieces and budgeted them for the day's meal. In desperation, I returned home and lived with my mother raising goats and chickens. My mother was my only barber, and I longed for the day when I could get a decent haircut without the straight rows and pinches left by the scissors.

I recall a Friday when my mother sent me to the nearby village to do some shopping and cautioned me to hurry back because it was time for my next haircut. Part of the shopping was done in a store right across from a barbershop. I could see the barber in his white apron and a rotating chair and electric clippers. I sighed and wished I could save myself the embarrassment of sitting between my mother's knees for another haircut. But I had no money.

On my way out of the store a messenger for the owner called me back. She gave me some money saying I had forgotten it on the counter. It was the exact amount for a haircut. Although I knew I had not left any money there, I took this as a gift from God for my long wanted haircut. I hurried to the barbershop and sat waiting for my turn. I pictured myself sitting in the chair, listening to the clippers run through my hair and, above all things, giving my mother that great surprise. I saw this as my day of liberty.

But for some reason I began to think about the change left on the counter. My conscience began to bother me with questions. Was that money really mine?

Was it really a gift from God? Was I certain I was not a thief? I felt like stopping up my ears, but it was not my ears, it was my conscience, and it was bothering me. I became very uncomfortable to the point where I was uneasy and could not maintain my composure. I got up and went back to the store and returned the money because the amount I spent there was the last I had. The lady, however, told me to take it because she could not account for it. I went back, this time fully convinced providence was working in my favor. The barber himself was delighted to see me back and assured me he would be with me soon.

This time my conscience reminded me of a young lady who had been in line before me. I recalled seeing her receive the change, which she inadvertently left on the counter. I hurriedly ran back to the store and related my story. Everyone was amazed at my insistence to return the money to its rightful owner. The manager was deeply impressed and took my name and address. I went home without a barber's haircut.

By the following Wednesday I got a telegram inviting me to come and see the manager of the same store. I was highly complimented for my honesty the previous Friday and offered a job as a manager of the store, starting the next Monday. When you are headed southbound, you become vulnerable to unfavorable circumstances, to undue pressure and situations that contradict your convictions, but you will not be deprived of the option of going northward, the highway to credibility, integrity, honesty, and trustworthiness. The southbound route is always shorter, easier, and less challenging. Many have taken it but found it less rewarding. It is always broad and crowded with multiple attractions, but it is a dead end with nothing but frustrations.

Westbound

Heading westward always brings to mind the setting sun, the end of another day and the beginning of another night. It gives the feeling of the time to close down work for the day, a time to relax and retire for the evening. It represents time to reverse thinking. I am reminded of a young man who promised his dad he would keep his promise this time and not go more than thirty miles from home, which was the round-trip distance from home to his grandmother's house. The last time he had borrowed the car, he had used up all the gas by driving to several places. But as soon as he turned the corner and escaped his father's gaze, he changed course, picked up his girlfriend, and just went driving. They spent the evening going several places. He seemed to have forgotten his promise.

The time came to head for home and face the fact that he had gone too many places. On checking the odometer, he discovered, to his amazement, that he had driven 225 miles. In desperation, he went to the nearest roundabout and decided to take the miles off. He put the car in reverse and drove in reverse, not realizing the miles were not going down.

An old lady who lived on the third floor of the nearby building heard the noise from this reversing car and, on looking through her window, saw this vehicle moving around continuously in reverse. She was frightened and called 911 to report the strange phenomena. The police, on arrival, managed to stop the car. They recognized the driver to be a teenager who was not under the influence of drugs or alcohol but was a troubled, frightened, and worried young man. On interrogation, the young man related his plight of the accumulated miles and his attempt to erase it. Smiling, the officer let him know that registered miles cannot be erased by driving the car in reverse. He had no choice but to face his father, acknowledge his fault, and face the consequences.

You may recall your own mistakes. You may be repining over your failure to achieve and blaming yourself or society. Don't try to reverse the damage, just shake your shoulders and try again or keep on trying. Heading westbound represents frustration, disappointments, and fear. You may be tempted to worry about what others may say, think, or do. Under such situations, you become a prisoner of circumstances. You become locked within your own feelings. You become a slave to the whims and wishes of others.

It may be your parents whom castigate you on the choices you make. They may monopolize your mind and feel their choices should be your choices. They may feel you should consult them in all your plans even though you are no longer a teenager. Don't get mad at them. They have your interest and well being at heart. Now that you are an adult, you probably should act like one and prove to them that your decisions are marked with maturity. But remember, as old as you are now, your parents are the equivalent in age above you. It will do you good and make them happy if you consult them. Of course, endeavor to maintain your personality and individuality. Prove to your parents that you respect and appreciate their decisions but that your taste and feelings differ. Your choice, though different from theirs, should not be observed as evidence of disrespect. *One can become so obsessed in trying not to hurt feelings that one ceases to exist as an individual.*

The westbound route carries a lot of negative signs: Steep Hill; Change to Low Gears; Winding Roads; Watch Out for Stray Animals; Accident Prone Area, Drive Cautiously; Slippery When Wet, Drive Slowly. Don't be a jellyfish; be yourself.

"I really want to be a doctor, but my parents say no because it costs too much and takes too long, so it is best that I give up that dream."

"I really love my girlfriend, and I want to marry her, but my parents don't like her, so I've decided to break up with her."

"He is the man of my dreams. He treats me like royalty, but my mother doesn't like him. He seems to understand, but some days he reminds me that a woman such as myself in my late 30s should be able to make her own decisions. I feel like a prisoner in my own life."

These are typical stories of westbound travelers. Westbound travelers are afraid to answer the phone when it rings because they are afraid to hear the message it brings. They are nervous and scared to open a certified letter because it carries an omen. They are afraid to call because the answer may be bad. They readily give up because they can't see the way. They do not see themselves surviving because help is not in sight and providence does not seem to offer any solution.

Eastbound

In the Bible we read about the wise men who came from the East because they saw the star. Thus, I suggest that heading eastward seems to indicate the rising sun or a sign of true initiative. At the beginning of a new day one generally looks to the east to see the rising sun. People who are pessimistic hate the rising sun because it reminds them of the miseries of the past or of yesterday.

I was early for class one morning, so I sat in my car and watched a man carrying a long bag on his back and a long rod in his right hand as he traversed the campus. I became curious about his activities because I noticed he was attracted to bits of garbage on the campus. I discovered his job was to keep the campus clean. The rod in his hand was a device for grabbing bits of paper and garbage, and the bag on his back was the receptacle for the garbage he picked up.

I then pictured some people as garbage collectors who pick up on the unpleasant situations on their day despite the many pleasant memories. They always recall the sad, unpleasant experiences: the mosquito bite, the mistake that someone inadvertently made, and the miseries of yesterday. They wish the weekend would never end, and they hate to go to work. Holidays are their greatest days because they can lie in bed and find the way to the refrigerator, their only itinerary for the day.

Eastbound gives you the courage to forget the past and the strength to press forward. People are always curious about someone attempting something new or attempting to do something that to them appears impossible. If your choice is to change from being a gravedigger to being an engineer, go for it. People who knew you as the famous gravedigger will see you as being too ambitious and may even laugh at you. Be proud and give them something to laugh about. If you are from a poor family and all your siblings have chosen ordinary careers, and you choose to be a lawyer, a teacher, a doctor, or a pharmacist, people may think you are crazy and may think you will never make it. Accept it as a challenge and prove to them that you can do it.

Chapter 11 Surviving Directions

Don't allow people with small minds to turn you around. Don't be afraid to be the first at something that is good. You are as big as you think. Don't allow your age, your color, your family background, or your financial status to be a barrier to achieving your goal. Be an initiator or an explorer so that others can follow. Prove to yourself and others that you choose to head eastward and are going to keep on rising until the day star accompanies you.

Be proud of being different. The mind is the measure of the man, which implies a man is as successful as he thinks he is. It's a matter of building confidence in you. Within every person lies the power to achieve. Achievement is the successful attempt to reach a goal. Your achievement is measured by the size of your projected goal. You will never achieve more than what you attempt. *Mismanaged negative imaginations breed fear, worry, tension, panic, and failure.* Fear negates opportunity and weakens one's vitality, which leads to lack of confidence and poor accomplishments. Confidence is not inherited but is acquired. Confidence is like swimming, it can only be achieved by action motivated by a willingness to overcome procrastination and indecision.

> **We should capitalize on isolating the cause for our failure and strategize to ind corrective measures.**

All failures have contributing factors, and finding out the causes will lead to finding the solutions. In an effort to build confidence, one will have to face realities with a mind focused on accepting tough challenges. We should capitalize on isolating the cause for our failure and strategize to find corrective measures. Don't memorize strategies. Use your brain to supply you with the resources and be prompt in using them. In the confidence building process, you will encounter unpleasant, discouraging, and frustrating experiences, but you should draw from your positive reserves so that such experiences will become steppingstones instead of barriers. One should stop magnifying past failures by not dwelling on them because memories of the past will color what you see in the present. When looking at other successful people, adopt the principle of also seeing yourself as successful, and be prepared to meet giant negatives with giant positives.

To enhance your confidence, endeavor to stand or sit with the crowd behind you. In other words, don't choose to stand or sit in the back. Choose to be a leader by trying to be in the front at all times if possible. Don't be afraid to introduce yourself or to meet people. A good handshake, accompanied by a brilliant smile, is a bulwark in building confidence. Your countenances, along with the pep in your step, are indices to the strength of your self-confidence, your attitude, and your behavior.

Convince yourself that you have an idea and force yourself to share it. Speaking up increases your confidence. However simple it may appear, try to be bold and join the discussion and express your opinion. You may think people will laugh at you and think you are stupid, but forego your impression and express it. You will find it easier to do it the next time a chance arises. You may not have a thought, but join the curiosity group and ask a question. In every group, you will find folks who suppress their thoughts because they lack confidence in themselves. Don't be one of them. Break the ice and speak up. *The depth of your self-confidence determines your survival, and this in turn measures the height of your achievement.*

The rising sun presents to every man moments consisting of minutes and hours decked with energy ready to be used. Every one of us has a right to a portion of this energy, and yours can be big or small. The size is determined by your thinking. The determining factor in your success is measured by the size of your thinking and not in inches, pounds, university degrees, or family background. *The size of your achievement is determined by the magnitude of your mind.*

One of our most frequent mistakes is found in how we rate ourselves. We have a tendency to underrate ourselves. When applying for a job, we are tempted to quote a very low expected income because we feel this makes it easier to be accepted. This is underselling ourselves. In presenting services, we are afraid to quote the right price because we feel it might be considered too high, so to get the job, we offer exorbitant discounts to our own detriment. People should seek you because you offer quality services and not because you are cheaper than others.

Single individuals, in their desperation and fear of not getting married, compromise their ideals and readily accept a contractual engagement that deprives them of the joy of a compatible and happy life. They need to be more selective in their search for a life companion. The idea that love is blind can only be true if this love is founded on infatuation. Too many times one is pressured into entering into a questionable situation with the hope that he or she is skilled enough to do so without being burnt. One offer deliberately ignores the risks and lowers his price tag with the idea that such an opportunity may not come again. Advertising goods for 99 cents has caught bargain hunters who eventually discovered they have been caught in a web of commercial gimmicks.

A young, intelligent professional woman sought my advice one day. She was depressed, frustrated, and bitter. She had fallen in love with a young man who had been a casual friend for many years. During those years, she did not see him as being qualified to be an intimate friend. Lately, she had become desperate for companionship and shifted the casual relationship to an intimate one. Circumstances forced her to cancel a date with this young man, and she became greatly concerned because she feared she might not be able to reconcile with him. She became so distressed and confused that she sought my council.

I reassured her that in most instances such disappointment was an opportunity to reevaluate a decision. She admitted that she was willing to take all chances regardless of the risks because she was desperate for companionship. I reminded her the worst time to make a decision that would influence her entire life was when she was desperate because in such a situation her emotional state would compromise her better judgment.

Two days later she discovered some characteristics in this young man that forced her to admit providence had intercepted the date. Since then, she has discovered a multitude of disqualifying attributes that convinced her this truly was the wrong choice. She now is rejoicing that unfavorable circumstances worked for her good.

When you become desperate, don't allow circumstances to force you to lower your price tag. *Always maintain the integrity of your better instinct.* Think big. People who are eastbound are always positive and full of praise. They continually speak warmly of their colleagues, companions, and family members. Their feelings are reflected in their face. One is measured by the way they greets others, what they say about them in their absence, and their description of their behavior. You should never allow your problems, frustrations, or disappointments to be reflected in your face. You are better off being seen as cheerful, courageous, and positive rather than downtrodden, failing, and forsaken.

When we remember we are a child of the King, we have plenty to be thankful for, and our countenance will display this truth. We are rich, for our Father in heaven has houses and lands and holds the wealth of the world in His hands. Eastbound travelers reflect the state of their minds in their faces. They are positive and emit sunshine in their paths. Regardless of the adverse circumstance, they give themselves a chance to believe they can make it. That which causes frustration, stress, and disappointment can be transformed into something that is exciting, productive, and rewarding. Just convince yourself it can be done, and your mind will create a way to do it. Solutions to all your problems, whether they be financial, social, or physical, generally follow your belief that there is a way out.

Remember, if the will to achieve exists, then the way will eventually show up.

Remember, if the will to achieve exists, then the way will eventually show up. Instead of concentrating on reasons why you can't, focus on reasons why you should. Feel bold to introduce changes to traditional thinking. You can reach where you want to go. Start an elimination process and begin getting rid of the negatives, such as thoughts that it can't be done, it won't work, it's useless trying, or it is impossible. Instead, tell yourself, it can be done, it is possible, it is worth trying, it will work, and I am going to make it. With this type of attitude, your mind will sustain the will to achieve and show you the way.

Some time ago I accepted a challenging contract to stem an epidemic that had been plaguing a country awhile. It was in a rural area with a population of more than 50,000. It had actually become a nightmare. No physician wanted to go into that area. I took the challenge and spent some time trying to find out the contributing etiological factors. My discoveries increased my enthusiasm. I then set up strategies that would comprehensively include preventive, curative, and control measures. These contradicted the traditional approach of gaining access to funding through grants and other methods of solicitation. My presentation was seen as impractical because of existing budgetary constraints. I devised a program that involved the entire community.

By motivating, stimulating, and educating the people, the burden of success was taken up by the community. We became a team, and some sixty-six community health groups were organized to see that the contributing risk factors were monitored, controlled, and eradicated. Up until that point complaints were stockpiled in the Health Department, and due to the limited staff and funds, most of the problems remained unsolved. Under the new approach, community members played a leadership role in implementing corrective measures on a voluntary basis. Thus, funding was not a problem. Instead of sending complaints to the office, the community was now seeking consultation on difficult issues and asking for tools, equipment, and other basic commodities to carry out their duties as volunteers. Through a united effort, the epidemic was cured, and the people continue to maintain the integrity of the program to prevent a recurrence. That experience proved that lack of funds does not minimize the ability to do something.

Traditional ideas and thinking can be barriers in ones ideas for progress. There is a tendency to feel that something that has never been done is impossible. The old traditional way of doing things has become the acceptable and any plan that falls outside of it is not worth trying. Eastbound travelers are not slaves to the old but are adventurers, seeking ways to improve, discover, and explore. Carriages drawn by six horses made a 100-mile journey in two or three days. Now vehicles with a six-horsepower engine can travel 100 hundred miles in ninety minutes. Columbus, Sir Francis Drake, Hawkins, and Ferdinand De Lesseps took months to travel around the world. Now luxurious ocean steamers traverse the globe in days. Your ideas may seem new and fanciful, but you can analyze, cultivate them, fertilize them, and then use them by transforming them into fulfilled realities. Traveling eastward gives you longer days with more sunlight for greater challenges and more opportunities. Dreams are short lived and sometimes forgotten. *If you have a dream, you can turn it into a vision and then into reality.* Eastbound travelers are aggressive, positive, and productive.

On the highway you often run into drivers who change lanes without thinking. They are always in a hurry, sometimes going nowhere. You may run into others who seem to be lost. They slow down to read every sign. They hold up traffic and get in the way of those who have a deadline to meet. There are others who are bewildered and confused. What about the student in the registration line who, on reaching the desk, is still oblivious as to the course of study he is pursuing? Eastbound travelers are focused and people see them as mature and organized. They are respected and represent the group that always gets the best job.

Those who are always heading for the bargain counter rarely attract the attention of salespeople. Likewise, the person who goes car hunting in an old beaten up car rarely attracts the attention of the salesperson because he is seen as a poor potential buyer. On the other hand, the man who demonstrates interest in the expensive jewelry, the man who is well dressed and drives up in a clean, expensive, well-polished car attracts a team of salespeople because he is seen as a potentially good client.

Your appearance is your number one selling factor. You should always make certain you look and act like the person you want to be. Always dress right and remember to see yourself as an important person. *Remember, people see you the way you see yourself. Your thinking serves as an index to your action.* Should you be going for an interview for an executive position then make certain you dress like an executive, speak like an executive, and act like an executive. You can't dress like a handyman and hope to be seen as an executive. A person's first impression is based on your first appearance and action, and this generally outlasts all other impressions.

On many occasions I have been given preferential treatment because of my appearance. If you choose to go otherwise, then you will find it twice as difficult to change the first impression that has already been made. People are more easily attracted to what is seen than what is heard.

Eastbound travelers specialize in quality rather than quantity. One will always be what he thinks he is, and society evaluates him accordingly as he is seen. On the eastbound route, you will reach as far and as fast as you think, and when you arrive, others will see you just the way you see yourself. On several occasions I set the alarm clock to wake me at certain time, but I found myself getting up before the alarm went off because the clock was slow. On those occasions my mind woke me on time because my mind is more reliable than the clock. Thus, whenever I am scheduled to travel by air or by land, I just register in my mind the time I want to be up, and however tired I may be and regardless of the time, I go to bed, and I am always up at the right time without the aid of a mechanical device. This may not be a unique experience.

Many have lost control of their minds and become drifters. Not having a mind of their own, they are solely controlled by others. They sometimes resort to the feeling of inadequacy with the idea that they were not cut out for certain things, especially those that demand sacrifice. Such persons are sometimes very talented but have developed a sense of insecurity based on fear and public opinion. They have a phobia of failing. They have become complacent with what they have, although it might be little or nothing. Generally, such people are influenced by friends who themselves are failures.

When you are on the eastbound route, you build up a defense against such people who try to convince you that you won't make it. You will see their negative advice as a challenge, inspiring you to make it. Aim at going first class regardless of how many friends or colleagues choose to travel second. First-class passengers are always treated better. Once you start on the eastbound way, you have survived the obstacles of the westbound route, and your adversities are behind you.

Chapter 12
Surviving Phobias

A phobia is a persistent, illogical, or abnormal fear of a specific thing or situation. Some people have a phobia of failure. They have never failed, but they have heard or read about some tragic result of failure. They become a victim to their own imagination. On reading about a plane crash, they imagine the flight they might be booked on will be the next flight to crash, and so they refuse to fly.

As a young man, I had a phobia of dead people. I would be very afraid after a funeral or when passing a cemetery at night. I saw imaginary ghosts and would actually experience extreme heat in my body, indicating that one was by me. One late night I had to pass by the tomb of two elderly folks who had recently died. Sitting on one of the tombs was a white creature with long upright ears, glassy eyes staring at me, and a body that was beyond description. I was spellbound for some minutes and was fully convinced it was the ghost of the dead man on whose tomb the creature was sitting. I was almost frozen and felt I could not run and should not attempt to move because the creature would outrun me if I tried to escape.

The more I looked, the more glaring the eyes appeared. After some time I began to recapture my thoughts and felt I needed to do something. I cleared my throat, and the monster shook its head and jumped off the tomb to be with its mother who was lying nearby. It turned out to be a young white goat kid. If I had left the spot without gathering my senses, my fears would have been perpetuated. *No one is immune to fear, but we should not succumb to it.* That kind of fear is a phobia.

While traveling on I-20 in Atlanta, I noticed I was being trailed by the flashing lights of a highway patrol car. Fear gave me quite a few suggestions to evade the police officer. I was more than certain I was up for a ticket. I pulled over, began to search for my driver's license, and nervously waited for him. You could hear the pounding of my heart some distance away. But when the officer approached, he did not pull out his book, nor did he ask me for any documents. He just wanted to let me know the door on the passenger side was not properly closed. What a relief. I heartily said, "Thank you, sir." So many people have died prematurely because of fear. And some have done questionable things because of it.

One evening on my way out of the hospital, I met a patient being carried by three men. I was forced to go back to the ward because of the apparent gravity of the situation. The patient was a fifty-five-year-old woman who had been diagnosed by her doctor as having cancer of the right breast. She had not eaten anything for several days and was deteriorating rapidly. I immediately ordered a biopsy and left for the weekend.

On entering the ward on Monday morning, I was approached by the supervising nurse and told the patient was near death. I immediately called the pathology lab about the biopsy and was told it was benign. I hastened to the patient's bed, and holding her by the hand, I introduced myself and told her that she did not have cancer. Surprisingly, she opened her eyes, and with a glimmer of radiating joy, she asked me to repeat what I said. This time she clasped my hand tightly, got up, hugged me, and shouted, "Thank you, Jesus."

She then asked the nurse for her clothes and walked out the hospital. It was unbelievable to see that a dying woman who had been so weak because she had not been eating could, on hearing such hopeful news, get up and independently walk out of the hospital. Indeed the mind is the measure of a person. In the Bible we are told of a centurion who invited Jesus to come and heal his servant who was at the point of death. On his way Jesus got another message from the centurion telling Him it was not necessary for Him to come because He could just speak the word and the servant would be healed. He reasoned that as a centurion he gave orders and they were carried out. On the strength of the centurion's faith, the servant was healed (Matthew 8:5–13). This concept of belief or positive thinking is called faith. We all need to capture this reality of positive thinking, because otherwise we are cheating ourselves of one of life's greatest assets. It is an indispensable ingredient to success.

Another phobia I lived with for twelve years was that of driving over a bridge called Flat Bridge. This bridge, as the name implies, crosses the Rio Cobre River, whose stream runs at the same level as the road for quite some distance. It had no protective rails because during the rainy season the river floods, and no rails have been able to withstand its force. The road makes a ninety-degree turn where it crosses the bridge. The turn is so sudden that it has become a burial ground for many vehicles. Engineers could not come up with any solution because the road and the river run alongside a mountain.

Chapter 12 Surviving Phobias

One Sunday morning I volunteered to go riding along this route with some cyclists. This was my first trip on this road, so I was oblivious of the river and the bridge. While the others slowed down to make the turn for the bridge, I ignorantly continued at the same original speed. In my attempt to make the turn, I was thrown off my bicycle into the rushing stream. Fortunately, one of my colleagues saw my plight and caught me by one of my feet and saved my life. It remained a lifelong nightmare, and for twelve years I dreaded the very thought of crossing Flat Bridge. I deliberately traveled a route that was twice as long to avoid it. It became my phobia.

Circumstances eventually forced me to travel that route. I had just picked up my new car from the wharf and was too tired to go the long way home. I invited a friend to ride home with me to stimulate my courage. He was not aware of my fear. When we were about one fourth of a mile from the bridge, I began telling jokes, which sparked laughter. As soon as we approached the bridge, I clenched my teeth, held my breath, and drove slowly over it. As soon as we crossed over, I parked the car and shouted, "We made it, we made it." That was the end of my phobia. It was no longer a nightmare. That route became my favorite, and I have since used it as any other without fear.

You may have a long history of failures that tempt you to believe that someone has put a curse on you. That is just an evil thought. Don't believe it, don't accept it, and don't allow it to weaken your determination to make it. And, by all means, don't allow it to push you to seek the advice of a spiritualist. Saul, the king of Israel, had so many defeats that he resorted to seeking the advice of the witch of Endor, and the results were calamitous (see 1 Samuel 28).

> **Wait on the Lord and be of good courage, and He will answer your prayers.**

Shortly after I had passed my local examinations, I lost my cap. Neighbors influenced my mother into believing some jealous enemy might have taken it to cause evil spiritual harm to me. She eventually succumbed to their suggestions and sent my sister and me to consult a spiritualist for protection. Fortunately, the spiritualist was on vacation, so we returned without any kind of help. The next day I found my cap under a tree where I had dropped it. I often wonder what would have been the judgment of the spiritualist about my cap and what protective measures she would have instituted if she had been home. When things are not moving the way we would like them to move, we should not allow our minds to mislead us. Your time, however long it may be, is but a moment in God's hand, so stop being in a hurry. *Wait on the Lord and be of good courage, and He will answer your prayers.*

Sometimes due to anxiety, people resort to following the daily horoscope. This can be very misleading. During my elementary school days, I celebrated October 28 as my birthday. I grew up accepting the predictions as given by my horoscope. I followed it in detail and felt every word was prophetic. It was during my college days that I decided to take a serious look at my birth certificate and discovered I was really born on October 5 not 28. This presented quite a transformation of predictions. If the former predictions matched my life, how was I to react to the latter? I had lived the first part of my life under a prediction that was quite contrary to the predictions as given then. I was reminded that we should not allow our lives to be influenced by what we hear, read, or see.

Fables are different from phobias, but if followed, they too can become a hindrance to achievement. Traditionally, if on your way out you should see a black cat it would be interpreted as bad luck. Some folks would, therefore, refuse to undertake any major business pursuit that day. However, a black cat running across your path should have nothing to do with your perspective on life. I have seen and passed many black cats, but all I saw was a cat. I remained focused and did not allow such a sight to influence my agenda.

Another fable that I remember from childhood is that if you point at a tombstone your finger will decay and fall off. Thus, children grow up with a constant fear of pointing at a tombstone. Some of these traditional beliefs may be extinct, but whether they are or not, in our efforts to achieve, unless we are focused, we can be easily dissuaded. The westbound experience does not have to be full of omens. It should prepare you for the rising sun. You will never arrive at your eastern destination if your face is turned westward. It takes a complete about face. Thus, if you feel your sun is setting, pause a while, make an about face and wait for your rising sun. It may take some time, but hold on and remember that the next sunrise is just around the corner.

Chapter 13
Surviving Love

"Beauty is only skin deep" is an old saying that is applicable today. Some of the most beautiful and handsome people have turned out to be the most abusive or miserable partners. *Love that is demonstrated is far more meaningful than one only expressed in words.* The eyes serve as an index of what is felt. Many times a person falls in love with someone because of eloquence in delivery, neatness in adornment, evident wealth, multi-faceted capabilities, a good profession, an elevated social status, or a friendly deed.

Love at first sight is generally founded on infatuation. It is a fact that certain things and persons are so attractive or magnetic in appearance that they draw others with a deep feeling of immediate satisfaction, but this type of magnetic pull is not enough to lead someone to a life commitment. I have read and personally know of marriages consummated after being in love for two weeks, but most of them ended in divorce within a year.

Some of the most eloquent speakers are specialists in making promises and building fantasies, but their lips reflect their minds while their hearts are rebelling. A shallow river has a lot of ripples that make a lot of noise, but a calm river runs deep. Actions speak louder than words.

Keep away from a person who continually refers to the first person pronoun and boastfully speaks of past accomplishments or projects on castles in a wonderland. Watch out for that one who sees you as a dream come true although he has never slept deep enough to have a dream. "I will do this for you. I will make you this, and I will give you that." Check on their background. Where has this person been and with whom? What castles have they built thus far? How many previous promises have been kept? Naturally you will not get the answers from this person. That is why one needs to be slow in making serious commitments. Sufficient time is needed to get some answers to avoid regrets.

One young lady fell in love with a young man who called her long distance twice every day. He promised to make her the happiest women in the world. Among the many things he promised to give her was a lovely home with all the associated luxuries. He was ready to marry right away and to have her move to live with him. She, however, chose to visit him before getting married. To her surprise, she discovered this eloquent young man had multiple prison records and did not even have a good job. Promises are comforting to fools, and such fools always choose to go where angels will not attempt to go. Don't be in a hurry. The bird that flies too fast misses its nest.

A person at church or at work may be quite a disappointment when seen at home. One needs to remember that sixteen out of every twenty-four hours will be spent seeing and dwelling with what was not seen when neatly dressed. Time in house clothes, when the face is unshaved or the hair is undone or there is no makeup, will help you see the real person you are in love with. Expensive gifts, a luxurious car, or a home in Beverly Hills are not true indices to measure the values of a person. True love is measured in quality and not by quantity. The token of love may be small and inexpensive, but the thought behind the gift will serve as an ingredient to your enjoying the same luxuries as an expensive home. There are a lot of fabulous homes and wealthy bank accounts serving as a veneer for couples that are miserable because they don't have love. There is always bickering, and the poor wife feels unwanted or unloved. True love needs no commercials.

Love founded on pure infatuation focuses on lusting after the person being loved. This makes one very kind and anxious to answer calls for help because there is a craving or an unquenchable desire to satisfy a sexual urge. These Samaritan attitudes many times serve as a cover and give the appearance of genuineness. Misinterpretation of such actions leads to an impression that may eventually seduce one into an intimate relationship that compromises one's self-esteem. It will take a while to uncover the deception. Thus, the commercials have succeeded, and the victim soon begins to suffer from remorse, depressive episodes, and a world of regrets. There will always be times of need when it becomes imperative to solicit help from your friend, but discretion dictates that one should limit the times of dependency so as not to become indebted and thus committed. Don't be too eager for help or too willing to accept offers.

Give your friend the opportunity to observe your independence. He will admire and respect you more for being what you are. One needs to be convinced that true virtue cannot be bought or sold and one can afford to say "no," or "don't," when there is an attempt to cross forbidden boundaries because there is no indebtedness for given favors.

One should always guard the values that set the price and be careful not

Chapter 13 Surviving Love

to lower the price tag. The most miserable feeling one can suffer is to look back on a broken relationship with regret for having given up too much to someone who does not merit it. It is always good to remember that dogs will always bite, pigs will always wallow in mud, and fire will always burn. Intimacy will never change the nature of the dog. Shortly after you have fed it, it will still bite. Bathing the pig and dressing it in white with a bow tie and rich perfume will not change its desire for the mud. So it is if one plays with coal. It will burn if it is alive, but if it is dead it blackens your hand.

Don't gamble with love. Don't exaggerate your expectations. Intimacy will not convert a deceiver into a saint. Don't compromise your integrity. Your self-esteem is all you have. It's your life. Don't lose it.

It is good to fall in love with a professional. It should offer prestige, financial security, social status, and a high level of independence. However, there are some basic issues, such as compatibility, that should be taken into consideration.

I knew of one situation where a teacher fell in love with her student. The friendship consummated in marriage. However, the husband still viewed his wife as his teacher, and she forced him to live with that thought. He had no share in the family affairs when it came to planning, financial arrangements or any major issues. He earned the money, but the budgeting was her duty. She continually hammered him with the idea that he was extremely fortunate to get a wife like her and she was his only chance. He was forced, because of his inferiority complex, to live a life of subordination. He felt inferior and lost the will to exist as a man. The marriage ended in divorce. There were some correctable mistakes made. The husband should have improved on his education even after marriage. By doing this, he would have eliminated his perpetual role as a student of his wife. The wife was encumbered with a superiority complex. This should have been discovered during courtship, but quite likely he was an average student being helped by a concerned teacher. It was unfortunate that such complexes forced each one to compromise the submission and respect they owed each other as man and wife.

When dating, it is important for both persons in the relationship to ask some worthwhile questions when it comes to the issue of marrying a professional. If the social and educational levels of one are much higher than those of the other, will the person in the lower level be seen as a shadow or echo of the higher one? Will one be seen and treated as lord of the other, or will each one see the other as a sweetheart? All these questions can be answered by being observant during the courtship period.

What about personality traits? One can be so peculiar, so picky, and so funny in all situations so that it is easy to see prejudice on display. Funny descriptions and slang terms aimed at family members by an admirer should not be overlooked. Do members of both families display compatibility? What about acceptance? It is not difficult to know and feel the warmth or coldness that comes with acceptance. The way parents and family members on both sides relate to each other are indices of acceptance. Sometimes prejudice is demonstrated in a very subtle way that depicts rejection and in order to avoid friction the person whose family is the culprit comforts the one who is offended by saying, "Don't let the actions or behavior of my family bother you. I love you, and that is what counts." The ideal situation presents a symbiotic atmosphere where both families work together to enhance a relationship that is binding and loving. Unless there is total acceptance by both families, barriers will impose on the well being of the marriage.

It is vain to think that how your parents feel about your lover does not matter. It is a fact that the Bible declares that for this cause one should leave father and mother and cling one to another, but it does not advocate separation on the grounds of prejudice. The Bible warns against being unequally yoked because of the unpredictable problems (see 2 Corinthians 6:14). I believe that this is not limited to religious concepts but also social status.

On the other hand, one should not go so low that it becomes a struggle to get up. Sometimes one falls in love with one whose culture compromises the ideals of true love. Such a person may be crude, immodest, discourteous, and thoughtless. They lack the finer attributes of a gentleman. They delight in calling to set up dates, but otherwise he has no time to call to show his interest in other concerns, such as asking how your day or night was, how lunch was, or whether you had a light or heavy day. They are always right and never admits to nor apologizes for any mistakes. One may live in hopes of training, refining, and making such an individual into the ideal, but such hopes never materialize. One's kindness can be misinterpreted and taken as a threat. Although one will never succeed in finding a perfect package, one should not exaggerate expectations. The leopard cannot change their spots nor the Ethiopian his color. Love is sometimes blind, but one can improve on their vision by using common sense. Don't allow your urge for a companion to bring you too high or too low. One is better off staying on middle ground than to live a life of regrets and remorse.

Courtship

A period of getting to know more about your admirer is known as courtship. This period entails days of frequent telephone calls and late night conversations. Questions provoke answers that provide family history, personal likes and dislikes, personal experiences, and projected goals and expectations. Here are some guidelines to follow in these telephone conversations:

Always keep in mind that someone might be eavesdropping and listening to every word of your conversation. Therefore, don't exaggerate or fabricate any statement that you would not enjoy disputing.

Imagine that your phone has been tapped and every word is being recorded. Are there any statements or comments made that you would be ashamed to hear again? Would you have used certain descriptions or made certain remarks about your previous lover or about anyone? Would you be as excited listening to the recording as you were when saying what you did over the phone? What statements would you have left out or what remarks would you have avoided? What about the jokes you made? Are they appropriate? Save yourself any regrets by not saying or making statements that you would not want repeated later on. Thus, be yourself and reveal it in your telephone conversation at all times.

As you talk, listen for remarks, descriptions, and statements made about previous boyfriends/girlfriends. Are they derogatory? What were the reasons for breaking up? How long did it last? How much blame does the speaker take? Do you have reason to feel the blame was unilateral, and if so, are you being seen as the perfect one who is immune to such described imperfections? Have you reason to wonder if you may be the next former boyfriend/girlfriend described to the person who succeeds you?

Listen to what is said about family life, home life, and parenting. How much emphasis is manifested in regards to a stable family life? Is the conversation focused on the obsession of being with you and physical affection? Do you talk about a real home, its atmosphere, its environment, tentative plans, goals for achievements, its timing and maintenance? What about children? How many are anticipated, when and how far apart? What are the feelings about personal family relationships? Do the parents play any significant role in the family? Bearing in mind that everyone is a replica of their parents, having received an equal share of chromosomes from father and mother, your offspring will also be a replica of you both. Thus, it's important to know something about family background and traits.

Talk about anything and everything you can think of. Are there any plans for future studies or educational pursuits? During your conversations, are their interrupting incoming calls? How is this handled? Are they unbearably long and are any explanations given? Are there times when calls are not accepted? If so, why?

After a long telephone conversation, have you discovered any conflicting thoughts that challenge your confidence? What is your true assessment of the person with whom you have been talking? Have you discovered the ideals of a mature, reliable, honest, and model companion, or do you have some reservations?

Dating

By this time you are now ready to meet each other on a date. Please bear in mind that the person you will be meeting on this first date will be putting his/her best foot forward. This person will be at his/her best, well dressed, well groomed, and wearing perfume. Remember this is the first impression. This person will be very polite, courteous, kind, and sweet. I heard the following experience of a first date:

The young lady was gorgeously dressed, and the young man was all you can imagine. They were both seated in the living room at the young lady's home sharing a glass of wine. In the middle of the conversation, the young man accidentally spilled some wine on the young lady's dress. She politely accepted the young man's apologies, smiled, and went to change her dress. Everything went well for the rest of the evening. After some months of courtship, they got married. On the first night of their honeymoon, the young bride brought out a pillowslip with the stain of her lipstick imprints. She reminded him of the night when he spilled the wine on her dress. She told him she had been so mad with him that she poured out her bitterness by biting the pillow. Then she remarked, "You got away with it that night, but don't let it happen again. Next time it will not be the pillow but you. Please remember this warning." It is normal to try to please the other people and put your best foot forward in the beginning, but make sure you know the real person behind the beautiful façade. Sometimes he/she may not be genuine.

The following are some specifics that one should not overlook. Are the dates progressively better or routinely the same? Are they somewhat exciting, unpredictable, or monotonous? How frequent do you go out and what is his favorite itinerary: your home, his home, a movie, a recreational park, or somewhere of your choice? Does it appear that he is afraid of running into someone or being seen with you somewhere? Remember this is a relationship you are hoping will develop into marriage. Are you satisfied with the attitude and behavior displayed? Are these traits representative of the type of companion you want to live with for the rest of your life?

Does he show any significant interest in special days like your birthday, Valentine's Day, etc.? Does he treat your body with respect and is he willing to wait? Is your integrity and reputation in tact or is it being ruined because of the relationship? If sound judgment leads you to dissolve the relationship, then you should have no remorse or regret over anything you did or said during the time you were dating. It is ideal if the breakup is mutual. It is also best if you part as friends and not enemies. It is important that neither party feels used or abused during the relationship or upon breaking it off.

Don't ever sacrifice your self-esteem to prove your love. A woman is like a rose. She is and will always be beautiful until virtue ceases to nurture her petals. A man is like the roots that supply the petals with virtue. When the roots are cut, the rose dies. Survival depends on living for one another and treating one another with gentle care.

Marriage

Most young people wonder when they should get married and to whom? The first man, Adam, was not given a wife until he was declared master of all the animals he had named and given a home in a pruned garden known as Eden. He also had a job to keep the garden well kept. So the ideal time to get married is when provision has been made for a home and its maintenance. This should not be an afterthought. One should not depend on the wedding gifts as the only source of household supplies, neither should he chose to live with the in-laws as a means to get married now before a home is established. A mutual understanding should be reached in advance so that after the honeymoon the couple can set up their home.

A wife should be a helpmate, not a maid. It is a misconception to think of marrying to fulfill the need for security or for someone to wash your clothes, cook your meals, bear children, and keep them and the house clean. It is far more reasonable to hire a maid to meet these demands.

It is not a coincidence that the first woman was not made from a bone in the head. Then she would have been responsible for all the planning and the overhead expenses. Had she been made from a bone in the hand then she would have been subjected to lifelong dictatorship. What if she had been made from a backbone? Then her rightful place would have been like a dog, walking behind the master who dictates, directs, and manipulates. Had she been made from a bone in the foot then she would have been subjected to abuse and disrespect without being annoyed. A bone in the side gives the wife her rightful place by her husband's side in all issues at all times, in sickness or in health, in poverty or in wealth, for better or for worse until death.

Keep your love well polished, and always endeavor to be at your best. The wife should endeavor to maintain her charm at all times so that her husband will always have reason to think about her. Her menus should be filled with surprises so that it will surpass the husband's temptation to eat elsewhere. Effort should be made to discover the likes and dislikes of one another in order to maintain mutuality at all times. Avoid being derogatory to each other, especially while around strangers. If the wife is being complimented for her beauty and comeliness by men, she can ward off seduction by saying, "Thank you. My husband continually tells me so."

Be inventive and work surprises into your marriage. Avoid preparing dinner the same way all the time. You can prepare the same food different ways in a different setting. Give him reason to avoid missing your meals because they are always well prepared and tasty. Refuse to go to bed without him so that he will be committed to be home on time.

The husband should be thoughtful and helpful. He should realize the wife's work at home is tedious. Thus, he should be willing to share in the housework, shopping, menu planning, cooking, and housekeeping. Little courtesies are like seasoning to a good meal. Always remember to say thank you after a meal, and compliment little changes that are made in the house and with the meals. Don't ever forget to mention your wife's beauty when she comes from the beautician or when she dresses for church.

Bring her little tokens when you are out, and remember to give her a call during the day to let her know you are thinking about her. Before you part for work and when you reunite, remember to embrace and kiss. Don't bark at one another; don't reciprocate bitterness. Treat her tenderly when she is blue. Always treat each other with mutual respect and gentleness in the bedroom. Talk together, play together, eat together, walk together, plan together, share together, pray together, sleep together, and live until death together. Be a model spouse in your aim of making your mate a model companion.

Chapter 14
Facing Realities

Your yesterday was the time when you fell in love, the time of your courtship. It was a time of excitement, anxiety, and anticipation. Those were the days when your companion was a star twinkling in the sky, a rose blooming with the morning dew, and a plum that was enticing to the taste.

While you were dating there were moments of anxiety when you wanted to hear the sound of a ringing telephone. There were moments of excitement when the long looked for time arrived to meet and be together. The exchange of tokens of love and tender touches and expressions were like the sunrise after a sleepless night. Fantasies were innumerable, hopes were high, and feelings were explosively deep with love. Life appeared like a fantasy and each felt that the other was a gift from the Creator and was indeed the reason for living.

Eating together was an exciting experience. Talking with one another, whether in person or over the phone, was sensational. Meeting and being together was revitalizing. Words spoken or written were well chosen and full of feelings. No one was as sweet, as beautiful or handsome, as heartwarming and romantic as one to the other. Dreams were full of passion. Nights apart were sleepless and moments were boring. Silence was distressing and absence was depressing. Anxiety changed into unleashed excitement when your yesterday became your today.

Today you are now together as man and wife, and somehow a lot of people forget about yesterday. Have you forgotten how to use the telephone? Is your star still twinkling? Has the rose lost its fragrance? Small tokens will not only bring surprise but memories. It is revolutionary to whisper words of love, to give a loving, tender touch that causes your morning star to twinkle. Do you fantasize sometimes and become explosively romantic? Do you still enjoy eating together, talking with one another? Are you still in love with one another? Do you still see each other as the most charming, the sweetest, and your real gift from heaven?

Contemplate these suggestions:

- Aim at making your marriage the most memorable, the most exciting, and the most rewarding in history.
- Spend time improving and multiplying the little things that contribute to mutuality and happiness.
- Keep watering your love every day or it will fade.
- Keep looking for the good in each other, and the evil will disappear.
- Whenever you see beauty or romance on the television or elsewhere, place your companion in the picture and start thinking about it. Should you see something that is missing in your thinking then try to supply it? Endeavor to see the beauty and fit yourself into the excitement with your spouse.
- Live and enjoy your today as if there will be no tomorrow. Your tomorrow can either be as memorable as or worse than your yesterday or your today. Although tomorrow may be only a promissory note in your hands, the key will be what you do today that opens the door. One's tomorrow is determined by how one lives today. Socially, it depends on the role one plays with friends, family, colleagues, and the community as a whole. If you adjust well, act well, and treat others the way you would like to be treated, then your tomorrow is scheduled to be favorably bright. One's family life can be a perpetually strong tomorrow if today the fundamentals of a good marriage are firmly established on mutuality, love, understanding, tolerance, and forbearance.

Procrastination can destroy the beauty of tomorrow. Expressions of love, tokens of appreciation, compliments, loving thoughts, tender touches, apologies, acts of forgiveness, and confessions should be done today and not tomorrow. The type of companion, the type of parent, the type of neighbor, and the type of community member you would like to be tomorrow should be seen today.

Your tomorrow can be full of remorse, regrets, disappointments, and frustrations if you continually take things for granted, avoid playing the role of a good partner, or refuse to abide by the common basics of a compatible relationship. Tomorrow, when it arrives, will always come following today and will always be a byproduct of today as today is of yesterday.

One's life is made up of the past, present, and future. The past comprises experiences that may be good, bad, productive, non-productive, or memorable. Whatever it may be, it should be a learning experience to stimulate growth, to motivate progress, and to educate for a better today. You should be able to make steppingstones out of failures and to transform the good into better and your better into best. Your present is a product of the past and can either be like refined gold or the dross that goes to the dump. Life is what one makes it. The future is in the hands of the One who promises a reaping according to one's sowing. The mirror does not change, it is the person seen in the mirror that changes. A person is a product of their mind and will eventually be what they want to be. Think about it. Make up your mind and be a survivor.

In the midst of living for today and looking toward the future, we often must cope with adversity and losses that threaten to tear our relationships apart. The rest of this chapter is devoted to stories about loss and strategies to deal with the challenges that we must face every day.

Losing Something You Love

Lobo was a Labrador retriever that I had grown to love. He was jet black, about three feet tall and weighed about 120 pounds. He was intelligent, well behaved, and lovable. He traveled with us from Jamaica to Atlanta to Mexico and back. On our trips to and from Mexico, we spent the night in a motel. During the night he would leave his bed in the closet and make his rounds, checking to make certain everybody was safe.

Every member of the family adored him. He enjoyed playing ball with the boys and hide-and-seek with my daughter. At night when he wanted to use the bathroom he would scratch on the door, and as soon as it was opened, he would run outside, do what he wanted to do, and rush back. He was a real protector and a proud member of the family. He refused to eat the crumbs that fell from the dinner table. He was a great dog and will always be remembered as the best friend the family has ever had. Then one day he wandered across I-20 in Atlanta and was hit by a car. We mourned his death as a missing member of the family.

Losing something or someone you have grown to love causes a lot of memorable flashbacks. Sometimes it leads to depressive like symptoms and, if not well controlled, will end in real depression.

Coping with losses can be a nightmare. It is very difficult to forget the time spent together with that pet or person. Loss of a friend, whether it be by death or by separation, has caused many sleepless nights, mournful episodes, loss of appetite, loss of self-esteem, physiological and psychological disturbances, social insecurity, religious instability, and mental imbalance. Time spent together will always come back to mind.

The question why will never be answered. Why did the relationship not work or why did this person have to leave when the relationship was so good? Was there something done wrong, expectations unfulfilled, something said wrong or misinterpreted?

Someone consulted me during a crucial time of loss. She had been friends with this young man for many years. She had occasions of mixed feelings, but because of her desperation for a fruitful relationship that would become permanent, she kept hoping that, in time, he would come to grips with himself and become refined, tolerable, and a courteous companion. Despite his aggressive attitude, she had maintained her self-esteem. After a long, unexplainable absence, he showed up and was extraordinarily nice. This time she went overboard to treat him nicely with the hope that this would stabilize the relationship into permanency.

She became excited and began to project toward a great future, but this was only a fantasy. After having a good time with her a few times, he forsook and ignored her for several weeks without any type of communication. Her attempts to contact him were all futile. This had been the worst experience she had ever had with him, more so after he had succeeded in getting her to compromise her scruples. She felt betrayed and worthless and became desperately frustrated. She confessed that a feeling of guilt had dominated her mind and that her life had reached a dead end. She was confused and sought my council to overcome suicidal thoughts.

This is a case of multiple and complex losses. She experienced the loss of hope, of a dream that never came true. There were thoughts of a home, a family, recreational activities, the excitement of romance, the thrill of having someone she could call her own and the beginning of a long looked for new life. All this was nothing but a dream. Not all dreams come true. Promises build up expectations, and this can be frustrating when they remain fantasies. Nevertheless, the unfulfilled promises should help one to reevaluate hopes and avoid dwelling too much on dreams. Most promises made during courtship are sometimes founded on emotions and never materialize.

There was also a loss of self-esteem. She regretted going so far and doing so much for someone who did not merit the sacrifice. She was encumbered with a feeling of dejection and began to feel that being meticulously selective was not important. I helped her to overcome such feelings of dejection and complexities. If a dog has bitten you once, you should be careful not to be bitten twice. If one plays with a coal, it will burn if it is hot and if it is cold it will blacken your hands.

This experience resulted in her losing confidence in men, which became a cornerstone in her life. There were flashbacks that would always bother her, but they helped her to be a better analyst of men's behavior. After some counseling, she stopped blaming herself for the mistakes she made in this relationship and decided to turn them into steppingstones One good for nothing man does not represent all men. There are good and bad men. If circumstances lead you to experience a bad one, take it to be a bad mistake. Turn around and remember the features of the bad one when your turn comes to make another choice.

She had a partial loss of mental stability. For some time she became grossly depressed. She was overcome with tears, sleepless nights, and a loss of appetite. It took a long time and some down to earth counseling for her to recapture her real self. If one falls into a mess, you do not have to sever the soiled limb from your body. All it takes is for you to get up, wash off the mess, and act as if you had never fallen into it. The disgrace is not in the fall but in the length of time it takes to get up.

She lost her appreciation for life and began to feel that a real curse had befallen her. She felt that God was punishing her for some wrong she had done. She lost her self-confidence, and desire to work and felt heaven had closed its doors against her.

In situations like this, one needs to recognize that God is not moved with vengeance or bitterness when one makes mistakes. The feelings or the pain one experiences after guilt are but consequences that accompany the wrong doing and are not to be considered punishment from a loving, compassionate God who will never close the door of opportunity to anyone. He is always ready to restore and replenish hope. His hands are always outstretched to lift you up. God permits consequences to help one realize the only safe path to travel is that which is the right way. You cannot trust the leading of your mind because it has been contaminated by evil.

> **God permits consequences to help one realize the only safe path to travel is that which is the right way.**

Losing a Loved One

Some twenty years ago I lost one of my sons in a motor vehicle accident. As our last child, he, at eighteen, had gained a prominent spot in our family of five. He was affectionately kind, handsome, and tolerant and was popular among all of his classmates. He was a dedicated Christian and held prominent offices in his church. He had just started his college career and lived with his sister in Atlanta, Georgia. He and two friends were en route to a church concert when they were involved in the accident. He and one of his friends died at the scene, and the third was hospitalized for some time.

At the time my wife and I were living in the Bahamas. We were overtaken with severe shock when we got the news. It took me a very long time to accept it. The question why kept ringing in my ears until I began to blame myself and feel that it was God's way of punishing me for some sin I had committed. I had certified so many deaths and performed scores of burial ceremonies, but I struggled to see myself grieving for a close member of my family. It became a nightmare until I came to grips with reality and remembered I was not sailing in a lonely boat—our whole family was sharing the same loss and bereavement. This thought changed my life, and I began to change my thinking and recognized that I should accept what I could not change and accept the loss as part of God's plan for our lives. Since He knows the end from the beginning and because He cares, He will allow only that which is for our own good. My daughter could have been dead too, because she had been scheduled to go on the trip but changed her mind at the last moment.

However bad a situation is, it could be worse. *In every situation one should always look for reasons to be thankful.* The loss of children, friends, or loved ones by death presents irreplaceable losses. The vacuum created by it can never be filled. Difficult as this may be, one should exercise implicit confidence in God who directs the affairs of His children. Our lives are in His hands, and He has promised that whatever He does or allows will always be for our own good. In other words, if we could see as far as He sees, we would have chosen to be led just the way He leads (see Romans 8:28).

The Loss of Something Very Valuable.

Five years after graduation from college, I acquired two lovely homes. This was done through hard work and great sacrifice. Shortly afterward I immigrated to the United States. Before I left, I rented one house to a friend and asked him to apply the rent as payment on a policy I had taken out on my children. He was the agent who had sold me the policy, so he agreed to make the payments from the rent. Six months later I discovered the policies were canceled because the premiums had not been paid since I left.

I canceled all arrangements with him and contracted another friend to collect the rent from both houses and apply a portion to the mortgage company on a monthly basis. I had taken out a mortgage on the second house but inadvertently did not subdivide the property so that both houses were on one title. After four months, I received a call from another friend informing me that the property had gone into foreclosure and been sold because no payments had been made for four months. Thus, in less than a year I lost the policies for my children and my two homes. Coping with this type of loss was more than a nightmare experience, although a very good teacher always carries expensive consequences. One should avoid taking things for granted. I should have subdivided the property and secured separate titles. That would have safe guarded against my losing both houses, as the mortgage was on only one.

When making grave commitments, one should think in terms of the unpredictable. Since spilled milk cannot be recovered, time should be spent in preventing the spill. If one contemplates committing an illegal act, one should not overlook the consequences of being caught. Likewise, when one plans to have illicit, unprotected sex, one should think of the chances of getting HIV, other sexually transmitted diseases or a baby. Moreover, when one closes one's eyes against parental advice, one faces regrets and incurable heartaches. If one turns one's back on God, then one is sure to reap the reward of the wicked and will be like the chaff that the wind drives away. Therefore, one should always think before jumping.

With my homes, I allowed myself to be bitten twice. Sometimes we put too much confidence in luck. We keep gambling with the hope that the next chance will be better. In the choice of a companion, we force ourselves to overlook the disqualifying mistakes with the feeling they were not too bad. We hope there may be some unseen good that will compensate for the bad. Evil, unless given up, can never be replaced by good. So we should never allow ourselves to be bitten twice by the same dog.

Furthermore, I compromised reality for friendship. It is vain to believe supposed friends will not deceive. There is a great difference between the friend who clings closer than a brother and one who gives because he gets. A true friend always treats his friend the way he would want to be treated. The absence of such a relationship resulted in my losses.

Losses, however valuable they might be, should not cause one to be mad with society. Instead, a full assessment of the contributing factors should be made. What is it that should have been done to prevent the unfavorable result? The answer to this question should help one establish strategies of recovery and preventive measures for reoccurrence. Losses, however, should enhance appreciation for success.

Losses sometimes are divinely ordained. The Bible gives the experience of Job who, within one week, lost everything, including his children and the support of his wife and friends. He consequently lost his health and went from being a multimillionaire to a pauper overnight. God allowed this challenging test to prove to Satan that regardless of such losses Job would not displace his trust or confidence in God. In this case, divine intervention restored Job's losses with superior quality and twofold in quantity.

Sometimes severe losses are lifesaving measures. One time when my family and I were returning to Mexico we got into an accident. We were driving a luxurious station wagon. This wagon was the talk of the town because of its style and color scheme. Two hundred miles from our destination, I ran into a Coca-Cola truck that was illegally parked near the edge of a hill. My insurance gave me the right to send my car back to the border for repair. It was a very frustrating experience to finish the trip without the comfort of my car. On reaching home, my nurse called and advised me to hide my car because the immigration officers were planning to seize it on the grounds that my immigrant status did not allow me to keep it. Despite the questionable nature of the charge, it was hard to know what would have happened, but God, who knows the end from the beginning, allowed an accident to take place so that my car would be returned to the American border to save it and me from harassment.

So it is that God sometimes allows circumstances to spoil our beautiful plans, which may, in a sense, be the dream of a lifetime, to save our lives. During the time when you are experiencing a loss, there will be moments of stress and sometimes depression. A strong religious background will help to change your negative perspective to a responsive attitude that will help you look for the derived benefits in contrast to the sustained evils around you.

Loss of Credit

We live in an age that survives on good credit. With good credit one has access to the comforts of life. Business thrives on credit, and one who has good credit becomes vulnerable to excessive debts as companies are prone to loan lots of money to someone who has good credit. One can move into a multimillion-dollar home with luxurious furniture, an expensive car and truck, a crowded wardrobe, and an expensive motorboat with a good credit rating. All this hangs on a good job with a reliable income. One's entire life hangs on good credit.

This becomes another story when one loses one's source of income and faces the reality of coping with the monthly reminders, the returned checks, the foreclosure notices, the frequent calls from bill collectors, and the dreaded loss of good credit. Applications for loans and for refinancing are all turned down because of derogatory reports from credit bureaus. How does one survive under such circumstances? Here are five suggestions if you find yourself in a financially challenging situation:

- Don't stockpile your reminders. Read them. There is always a number to call and explain. Most creditors are tolerant and will accept a justifiable explanation.
- Foreclosures can be negotiated. Mortgage companies are always willing to offer reasonable options. Don't panic.

- Disconnections are negotiable. Call the company and follow their recommendations. Remember, you are not the only one receiving such a notice. Don't be like the foolish ones who give up and face disconnections.
- Don't avoid answering the phone. The bill collectors are being paid to call you in an attempt to collect. Talk to them and negotiate. You don't have to accept their options if you can't meet them. Make your offer and let them know the circumstances surrounding it. Generally they will accept them because it enhances their rating.
- Don't resort to living off unemployment benefits. Try hard to find a job. You may have to resort to temporary employment until you find the right job. Such a move will enhance your rating with your creditors.

Loss of credit can be disastrous, but being down today offers you the challenge of being up tomorrow. Aim for it.

Loss of a Job

The loss of a job can be a challenging experience. A paycheck is like the bloodstream that supplies nourishment to the entire body. Depositing a check to the checking account gives one the glimmer of hope to face the incoming bills with a smile. It makes one feel good to be able to sit down and write a check with confidence that it will not bounce. Losing a job deprives one of those feelings of independence and brings in stress and anxiety. Coping with such a situation may include the following:

- Endeavor to make the job-hunting period as brief as possible by being aggressively persistent.
- Have an updated resume.
- Be prepared to take what you can get until you get what you want.
- Make certain to inform all your creditors and arrange for a relaxed payment schedule.
- Adjust your budget to accommodate your available cash and eliminate the extras.
- Shop selectively.
- Cut down on credit card purchases and unnecessary trips.

Loss of Your Good Name/Your Credibility

A good name far exceeds great riches in value. A lot of things go together to make up a good name. When one consistently keeps their promises, they build up confidence in the minds of those with whom they do business. This may relate to keeping appointments, paying bills, or being a good, reliable worker or just an honest, truthful citizen. One who cheats, lies, steals, or borrows without paying back loses credibility. People become afraid of them and hate the idea of doing business with them. Effective corrective measures can only be implemented by the guilty individual, which necessitates a strong willpower and determination to do better.

Earlier I told the story of two men who were caught stealing sheep. Although both men were branded in their forehead with the letters S.T., standing for sheep thief, the one man chose to change his reputation by living an honorable life. And he succeeded! Within time, people forgot what the abbreviation stood for, and one tour guide suggested it stood for saint. Thus, the man turned his reputation around with hard work and determination.

It is a common tendency to live in fear of public opinion. Church members who have committed a mistake often stay away from church because they feel all the members will be saying derogatory things about them. They avoid social occasions and are hesitant to strangers. They become suspicious, pessimistic, and secluded.

Some worthwhile suggestions:
- Live today and forget yesterday. However bright or dark it might have been, it is a canceled check. The mistakes committed are forgotten unless they are recalled. As a boy, I was annoyed at a caterpillar that I caught eating the buds on my blooming tomato plant. In my rage, I locked it away in a jar with the hope of watching it die slowly. However, I was shocked to find it turn into a beautiful butterfly. I had hated the caterpillar, but I knew that the butterfly would be good for my garden and would pollinate my plants. One day's frustrations or failures give way to a brighter tomorrow.
- Be positive in all your thinking, actions, and attitude. Give yourself a new perspective. Live and act like the person you really want to be. Surprise the pessimists. Disappoint those who criticized, condemned, and hated you. Be your real self, and stop worrying about the impressions of others. Talk to the person you are seeing in the mirror. What are some of the disgusting features you see in your reflection? Give yourself some advice as to how you can replace them with better features. Make a commitment to yourself. No counseling or discipline is as effective as the commitment made by one to themselves.

- If you have been the victim of bad influence, change your company. Mix and associate with people of honest report. Change your name. Be a Christian. However vile you might have been, take the name of Jesus with you. It will give you joy and gladness. It will carry you through. This change will give you a new passport to life.
- Don't discuss your past with anyone. Don't try to offer an excuse for the mistakes of the past. Bury them and place a tombstone on them with the words forgotten forever.

A painter was contracted by a church to paint a picture of Christ. He walked various streets looking for a man who would give a true picture representing Christ. He eventually ran into a well-dressed young man going to church and offered him $50.00 to sit for a few minutes as he painted his picture. When completed, it was a beautiful replica of Jesus. Three months late, he was again contracted by the same church to paint a picture of Satan. He walked the streets again and ran across a drug addict. He was unshaved, dirty and ugly. He paid him $50.00 to paint a picture. When completed, the painter Informed him that he had just painted a picture of Satan. The man began to weep with bitter tears and told him that three months before, he had been painted by him as a true replica of Christ. It is amazing what changes are brought about by the person whose name you carry. One who has made a complete right about turn is never asked where they are coming from but more so where they are going.

The Bible provides some reassuring promises as to the right course that one who has done something discreditable should take:
- When you confess your mistakes (sins) to God, He will forgive you and cleanse you (see 1 John 1:9).
- Although your mistakes (sins) be red like crimson, God will make them as white as snow (see Isaiah 1:18).
- When God forgives your mistake, He throws them into the bottom of the deepest sea and remembers them no more (see Micah 7:19).

In God's sight, mistakes are not rated as great or small, nor as dangerous or safe, but as sins. The best thing to do about them is to acknowledge them, confess them, and avoid repeating them. Some good examples are:
- Peter denied Jesus by cursing and swearing, but he was forgiven and became the great evangelist at Pentecost. As a result, 3,000 souls were baptized. He was converted from one who denied Jesus to a great preacher (see Acts 2:14).
- Jacob, the robber and professional cheater, became Israel the overcomer (see Genesis 32:28).

- Saul, the hated persecutor and murderer, became Paul, the devout missionary and a prolific gospel writer (see Acts 9).
- Rahab, the prominent harlot of Jericho, became a prominent figure in the faith hall of fame (see Hebrews 11:31).
- Mary Magdalene, the prostitute, became the first missionary to announce the glad tidings that Christ had risen from the grave (see John 20).
- David, the adulterer and murderer, became a man after God's own heart and was accepted by God as His servant (see Psalm 51:3).
- In the New Jerusalem, the great multitude will sing the song of Moses, the deliverer and the Lamb who forgives and forgets our sin and washed us clean in His blood (see Revelation 14:1).

Therefore, don't worry about yesterday with all its mistakes, but be happy for today.

Loss of Self-Esteem

A lot of good people with good intentions, high ideals, and good character have had experiences that led them to lose their self-esteem. The woman caught in adultery was not deliberate in her behavior, but she was a victim of deceptive abusers. A lot of good women have been caught in situations that on the surface are unavoidable. Promises and misconceived actions appear so convincing that grave decisions are made. The individual is led to believe it was worthwhile to take a chance. Deep down is a hope that despite the disqualifying features, there are some unrevealed good values that are worth venturing for. It is a dream that since every one of us has some predisposing evil that beclouds the hidden good maybe it is worth compromising principles with the hope that good will displace evil. When such dreams are not realized, the individual faces a delusion that at times lead to a loss of self-esteem.

In this situation one finds oneself taking a lot of things for granted. You lose your desire to work, to be selective in your choice of friends, to aspire for personal improvement, to mix or associate with friends, to trust anyone, or to be involved in social activities. You feel that you are worthless, rejected, and dejected. You possess negative thoughts and begin to associate with questionable characters.

Some coping techniques:
- In his attempt to deceive, the culprit sometimes uses a good trait to disguise evil. He may temporarily become very kind or courteous to be convincing. He tries to show some evidence of reform. One, in turn, becomes overly surprised at such marvelous changes, not realizing they are but deceptive devices. Should one become a victim of such a scam, you should not blame yourself. *You should review all oversights and reevaluate all miscalculations, analytical mistakes, and misappraisals and capitalize on them as learning experiences and steppingstones.*
- Having been bitten, you should now be wise enough to know vipers and be able to avoid being bitten again. Use your expertise as anti-venom and be happy you survived. One who never made a mistake has achieved nothing, so don't be discouraged. Remember the slogan, "Though I fall I will rise again."
- Isolating yourself weakens your ability to survive another attack. In your state of dejection and rejection, you become more vulnerable to the whims and wishes of other vipers. More glorious promises will seem enticing. One will soon be saying, "I could never treat you the way you were treated. You are too nice to have been mistreated, abused, and neglected. Give me a chance, and I'll prove I am better." The serpent made promises like these to Eve, and she was deceived. The consequences have impacted all of us. Rise up and surprise the deceiver. Recapture your composure and reclaim your self-esteem. You are of high price and have what it takes to be the person you really want to be.
- This might be a good time to change your environment and become involved in some higher educational pursuit or a new job. This step would give you an opportunity to make new friends, to have fewer flashbacks and would provide an easier chance to regain your identity and self esteem. Something new always offers new aspirations and new perspectives.

- Don't be in a hurry to fall in love. The scars are still tender and painful. On a whole you will be a little too critical, suspicious and fearful. Give yourself some time for complete healing. Be sociable but very selective. Maintain a healthy, charming and winning profile. Someone out there is searching and praying hard to find you. Just be patient, ardent, and prepared. The best fish generally comes from deep waters, so don't hang around the shallow waters if you are searching for good fish. Remember, good things come to those who wait.
- Coping with loss will take time. One may have concerns about some of the consequences or experiences. Occupying yourself with activities that are uplifting and recreational will fill the vacuum and relieve the mind of the flashbacks. Everything in life comes in pairs. Likewise, every synonym carries an antonym, e.g., light/darkness, good/bad, happiness/sadness, and gain/loss. If one is not gaining, one is losing. Thus, if one is losing then one's next move is guaranteed to be gaining. It is reassuring to know that since you have recently sustained a loss, this should be reciprocated by a gain. The time it takes to transform a loss into a gain is determined by the way you handle your loss. Give yourself a fair chance. Don't lower your price tag. You are not on sale. Go first-class and demand your price.

Chapter 15
Yesterday

Let's join hands and take a walk retrospectively into the past. This may take us back years or months, but it will give us a chance to review the pages covering the experiences you had before you reached where you are.

Think of the many questions you had to answer when you contemplated changing your status educationally, financially, socially, and, probably, spiritually.

There was the question of how would you make it, where would you find the resources, and when would they be available. From the mere fact that you are where you are today, it seems you found the answers.

In looking back on yesterday, can you recall the many imposing barriers such as financial restrains, peer pressure, age conflicts, social barriers, and the many, many other roadblocks your confronted that almost made you change your aspiration?

What about the struggles, the frustrations, the sleepless nights, the sacrifices, the deprivations, the losses, and the associated heart arches and headaches that you encountered in your effort to achieve your goal?

On the other hand, you might not have had any such experiences because you were blessed with inherited resources, which relieved you of the struggles the less fortunate had.

In courtship, you might have encountered misgivings or utopian promises that, one way or the other, motivated you to take the marriage vow.

Yesterday was a time when you fell in love. Yesterday features days filled with tense moments when you were waiting for the phone to ring and to hear that sweet voice at the other end of the line. Moments of excitement filled the air when you met and embraced each other. The exchange of tokens of love, tender touches, and expressions were like sunrise after a sleepless night. Hopes were high and feelings were full of love. Life ceased from being drab and each felt the other was a gift from the Creator and was indeed the reason for living. Anxiety changed into unleashed excitement when yesterday became your today.

Today

Today stands midway between yesterday and tomorrow and should in fact be a product of yesterday. In essence, it should be a true reward for sacrifices made, frustrations encountered, and goals achieved. Today you should either be better than you were yesterday or the same. *If you have not achieved your goal, it may be that you need to change your technique, your methods of thinking, your approach, or your environment.*

Don't discredit yourself for having not achieved yet. Some of the world's greatest achievers succeeded after years of seeking, trying, and exploring. Should your today reflect achievement and success that fosters joy and delight, then congratulations. Keep on looking in the mirror and promise the person you see that you are going to keep on climbing until you reach the top of the ladder. Your today will soon be your yesterday. Don't let the dark spots of yesterday conceal the brightness of today. You merit your achievement; it's yours, guard it well and be proud of it. Don't let this be your last achievable goal. Keep on climbing until you are satisfied you have reached the top.

> **With inner con idence and hope in God, you can overcome any adversity and enjoy success.**

By the way, if today means that your love has materialized into marriage and you are together forever, what about the flashbacks to yesterday? Has your star lost its twinkling nature and the rose bud its aroma? What about the romantic statements you used to make, the expressions of love in your secret telephone conversations and the joy you had when you met? Have all these been forgotten? The most delicate petals will fade if they are abused and handled roughly. In this instance, your today should be a continuation of your yesterday. On the other hand, if your yesterday had some shortcomings, you can use today to start corrective measures. Today is your paycheck. Sign it and spend it. It is yours to keep and enjoy.

Tomorrow

Tomorrow is the day that follows today, and as long as there is a today, there will always be a tomorrow. One is separated from the other by a night so that each is independent of the other. They are separate entities, and love will always be so. Transforming your goals into achievements can easily make your tomorrow into your today.

Tomorrow encompasses the negatives: I don't know, I may, I hope, I wish or maybe. Transposing the negatives, forces one to say, "I know I can, I will, I know, and I am. Spending time to improve, to grow, and to be better today will help to make your tomorrow a continuation of your yesterday. Be true to yourself and your hopes and dreams. With inner confidence and hope in God, you can overcome any adversity and enjoy success.

A Special Chapter
Surviving Some Health Issues

Along the eastbound highway some enthusiastic traveler may inadvertently encounter some unexpected adversity in the form of illness. This fosters discouragement, frustration, or depression and may cause some to feel that they have come to the end of the road. Thus, knowing the etiological contributing factor causing the ailment will accentuate a desire to turn this status into a steppingstone.

As a young man I caught the caterpillar that during the night had eaten all the leaves of my young tomato plant. In my rage I placed it in a closed jar for it to die. To my surprise a few days later it had transformed itself into a beautiful butterfly. It had gone through its pupal stage.

Illness can be transposed and used as the pupal stage for new discoveries for higher service.

The Braille system was the pupa stage resulting from blindness. A prosthetic devise is the pupal stage resulting from an amputation. No one is immune to adversity, and so if one should suffer from a disease because of bad genes, a germ, or an accident, one should focus on converting it from being a barrier to finding options that accentuate opportunities for reaching your goal to serve. A dark night increases your delight in a cloudless day. In our world today *there are those who are afflicted by disease but, in their zeal to achieve their goal, have found alternatives for survival.*

Surviving Aids

Acquired Immune Deficiency Syndrome (AIDS) is a disease caused by the Human Immune deficiency Virus (HIV), which attacks the body's immune system. The body, under such attack, becomes vulnerable to diseases and finds it very difficult to respond to the best of treatment.

One gets the disease by:
1. Having unprotected anal, vaginal, or oral sex with an infected person.
2. Sharing needles and syringes for injecting drugs with an infected person.
3. Children born to infected mothers can contract the disease during pregnancy.

The following are also risk factors for contracting the disease:
1. Homosexuality
2. Promiscuity with prostitutes
3. Multiple sex partners
4. History of having gonorrhea syphilis or herpes
5. Sexual exchange for drugs or money
6. History of sharing needles for drugs
7. History of receiving blood products or a transfusion between 1977 and 1985
8. Being a heterosexual in a country where AIDS is common in heterosexuals

Tests are accurate if done at least three months after the suspected time of infection. It takes an average of eight years for symptoms to develop, so healthy looking people can be carriers of the virus. Thus, it is very risky to take chances. One does not get the disease by casual contact: touching, shaking hands, hugging, swimming in public pools, giving blood, using hot tubs, public toilets, telephones, door knobs, water fountains, food, mosquito bites, or other insects.

For those not abstaining from sex or not in a monogamous marriage relationship, the safest course to follow is to practice safe sex by using latex condoms or contraceptive cream with spermicide. The spermicide should be put in the vagina rather than just in the condom. Condoms should not be reused.

More detailed information can be found at *http://1ref.us/7x*

Surviving Alzheimer's Disease

This is a mind wasting disease that afflicts as many as five million Americans. It destroys brain cells and robs a person of memory and reasoning powers.

The following are risk factors of the disease:
1. Circulating problems stemming from high cholesterol and high blood pressure.
2. A history of small strokes.
3. A family history of Alzheimer's disease.

Although there is no sure way to prevent the disease, some of the following tactics might help reduce the risks:
1. Always use bicycle helmets and seat belts and slip proof shoes to reduce the chances of injury. Head trauma is linked to a higher risk of Alzheimer's.
2. Exercise regularly.
3. Eat a low fat diet rich in vegetables and fruits to keep your cholesterol low.
4. Avoid being overweight. Obesity triggers diabetes, which is a risk factor for Alzheimer's disease.
5. Get sufficient levels of folic acid and vitamins C, E, B6, and B12.
6. Stay mentally active, read daily, play games such as chess, dominoes, bridge, cards, do crossword puzzles, or some correspondence course.
7. Play music.
8. Mental and physical activities appear to boost the release of substances in the brain that may help repair damaged tissues.
9. Go for a walk regularly.

More detailed information can be found at *http://1ref.us/7y*

Surviving Diabetes

Common Risk Factors	
Type 1	Type 2
A strong family history of Type 1 diabetes.	A family history of diabetes
Caucasians are prone to having this type.	Limited regular exercise
	Obesity
	Hypertension
	High cholesterol
	Being age forty-five or above
	History of diabetes during pregnancy (gestational diabetes)
	Greater risk for African Americans, Asian Americans, Hispanics, Pacific Islanders

Diabetes causes sugar to build up in the blood and thus prevents the body from using food in the most effective ways. Without treatment, this can lead to a number of serious long-term health problems. This disease affects some sixteen million Americans today. There are two major types:

Type 1 Diabetes: The body is deprived of sufficient insulin to break down food into usable energy.

Type 2 Diabetes: The body is unable to use insulin effectively. This is the most common type found in adults who are overweight. A lot of people with Type 2 do not even know they have the disease.

Warning Signs	
Hypoglycemia (Low Blood Sugar)	Hyperglycemia (High Blood Sugar)
If not treated can lead to loss of consciousness	In this state, the patient can go into a diabetic coma
Feeling cold or clammy	Dry mouth
Nervous or shaky	Increased thirst
Very hungry	Fruity smelling breath
Weak	Dry flushed skin
	Loss of appetite
	High sugar levels in blood or urine
	Excessive urination
	Labored breathing

Following are symptoms of Type 2 diabetes:
- Frequent urination, especially at night
- Increased thirst
- Increased hunger
- Blurred vision
- Fatigue
- Weight loss
- Sores that do not heal

The following steps, if observed, can help to control diabetes:
- Eat a balanced diet, low in fat, moderate in protein with plenty of vegetables and fruits.
- Follow a program of regular exercise (aerobics or brisk walking)
- Lose some weight. For men, the standard weight should more or less be 100 pounds for five feet in height, and then add six pounds for each additional inch. For women, do the same, but add five pounds for each additional inch.

More detailed information can be found at *http://Iref.us/7z*

Surviving Colon Cancer

Colon cancer is America's #2 cancer killer. This is a disease that affects an equal number of men and women, especially those over the age of fifty. It can also be found in younger people who may have a family history of colon cancer or other digestive diseases. This is one of the few cancers that can be prevented.

Everyone over age fifty should have:
- A screening test for cancer of the colon
- An annual fecal blood test for occult blood
- A sigmoidoscopy every five years
- A colonoscopy every ten years

The following are risk factors of colon cancer:
- Personal family history of colon cancer
- Family history of polyps
- Family history of chronic digestive problems such as Crohn's disease or ulcerative Colitis

Early stages of the disease present no symptoms; therefore, if you experience any of the following, you should immediately see a doctor:

- A change in bowel habits (diarrhea, constipation)
- Rectal bleeding
- Bright red or dark blood in stool
- Stools that are narrower than usual
- Frequent gas pains, general stomach discomfort (bloating, fullness, cramps)
- A feeling that the bowel does not empty completely
- Loss of weight for no apparent reason
- Constant tiredness

The following is a list of recommended screenings for various risk factors:

1. Average risk – People age fifty or older with no risk factors should have a colonoscopy every ten years or a sigmoidoscopy every five years, plus an annual fecal occult blood test.
2. Moderately increased risk – People with a family history of diagnosed colon cancer at age sixty or older should have a colonoscopy at age forty and once every ten years, or a symoidoscopy every five years with annual fecal occult blood test.
3. Moderately increased risk – People with a family history of diagnosed colon polyps earlier than age sixty should have a colonoscopy beginning at age forty or five years younger than the age of diagnosis for the youngest affected relative, and every three to five years, depending on strength of family history and findings of colonoscopy.
4. Higher risk – People with more than one member of their family with diagnosed colon cancer before age sixty should have a colonoscopy at age forty or ten years younger than the age of diagnosis for the youngest affected relative and every three to five years.
5. Highest risk – Familial polyposis or hereditary nonpolyposis colon cancer should be referred to a specialist. Remember to prevent is ten times better than to cure. So don't wait for symptoms because it may be too late. The best time to get a checkup is when you are feeling well.

For additional information please visit *http://1ref.us/80*

Surviving The Weight Problem: Obesity

Most cases of obesity are due to physical inactivity and excessive food intake. It can also be caused by endocrine complaints. This type is generally caused by a sudden onset that is associated with lethargy and urinary frequency.

Obesity can be described as a 10 percent increase above normal weight, which is generally due to deposits of fat in the body cells. Body build, musculature, familial, and socioeconomic tendencies are strong determining factors. About 50 percent of Americans are considered overweight. From a metabolic point of view, obesity can be considered an intake of more calories than are required for daily energy output.

- There are two types of obesity based on the number as well as the size of the fat cells. The hypertrophy or adult onset obesity represents the adult with a normal fixed number of fat cells who gains weight by depositing fat, which causes these cells to increase in size. Such obesity is amenable to weight reduction.
- The hyperplastic type of obesity involves increase in the number and size of fat cells during childhood. This kind is difficult to lose or maintain.

Obesity is associated with increased morbidity and mortality. People who are obese are liable to have hypertension, diabetes mellitus, gallbladder disease, gout, and heart disease. Other possible consequences are cancer of the breast, the endometrium, gallbladder, and colon as well as hazards in pregnancy and surgery. The standard acceptable weight can be calculated as follows:

- Men: 100 pounds for the first five feet in height and six pounds for each additional inch. Thus, a man measuring 5 feet 10 inches should weigh 160 pounds. Body build and musculature will cause some deviation for more or less.
- Women: 100 pounds for the first five feet in height and five pounds for each additional inch. Thus, a woman measuring 5 foot 10 inches should weigh about 150 pounds depending on body built and musculature.

The body needs carbohydrates, proteins, fat, vitamins, minerals, and water to meet the demands for daily activities. A balanced diet is made up of all those components in proportions. Carbohydrates and fat provide energy for the physiological and organ function. Vitamins, proteins, and minerals are body builders and regulators. Water provides the liquid mainstay for all mediums by which the foods are transported and transformed into the nutritional and physiological needs of all the systems making up the body. When the energy input exceeds the amount the body needs for its daily output, the excess is stored in the cells and causes a bulging of the cells. If the stored fat is not used in energy output through activity and additional intake continues to be stored, the bulging cells will gather in the most conducive areas, such as the abdomen, buttocks, legs and, waistline until the whole body becomes a complete bulge. When it reaches this stage, closets or wardrobes have to accommodate new outfits with wider waistlines and bigger bust lines, and the budget gets tighter and slimmer. When such a big bulge looks in the mirror, it wonders who and what it is, and worry takes over. Mr. Slim Fast comes in, and diet pills and diets make life a misery. Anxiety takes over because the bulging shape makes one less attractive, less active, less motivated, less healthy, less sensational, and more dejected. The extra weight did not develop overnight but is the result of saving unused fat over the years. It would therefore be unrealistic to get rid of it overnight. The wisest course to follow would be to prevent it. Learn how to avoid taking in more than you need for your daily activity.

- Be selective in your eating. Strive for quality, and not quantity.
- Be health conscious. Eat three balanced meals a day. Avoid snacking.
- Exercise regularly at least three times a week.
- Be alert. Watch out for excess sugar (cookies, pies, ice cream, and cake); be moderate.
- Keep a positive outlook on life. Keep a healthy mind.
- Keep up with your annual physical checkups.

The following paragraphs provide some hints on losing weight. In weight gain, the body does not gain an increase in the number of cells but rather the cells get larger due to fat deposits. The fat in these cells is the body's way of conserving excess for hard times. It was not intended to be there indefinitely but to be used up in time of need.

Daily requirements of energy vary according to the day's activity. One who sits at a desk all day typing or dictating requires fewer calories than one who works at the plow, a sewing machine, or in a carpentry shop. Thus, caloric needs can be compared to a checking account. Checks drawn on the account represent the daily caloric needs. Balance brought forward represents the fat reserved in the cells. To avoid a cash balance, checks drawn must be equal to the exact amount deposited. In other words, your intake should be equal to your energy output. Should you need 2,500 calories to keep your mind planning and your fingers punching at the computer every day but consume 3,500 calories instead, by the end of the year a huge savings in the form of fat has been made, possibly with a visible ten pounds or more in the buttocks or thighs.

To be petite or well built so as to be agile, flexible, and pleasing, extra activity in the form of exercise must be done to use the reserved fat. To maintain a true balance, an intake of 1,500 calories will force the body to use up 1,000 calories from its reserve. If this is done on a voluntary basis, the body will accept it without seeing it as a deprivation. By knowing the caloric value of foods, you can eat whatever the appetite calls for (be it chocolate cake, ice cream, apple pie) as long as it does not exceed the desired 1,500 calories daily. This 1,500 is divided into three meals that are nutritionally balanced. Make certain each meal has the equivalent amount of calories for the activity that follows. Thus, the period of the least activity should follow the meal of the fewest calories. If your meal is balanced, meaning it meets the body's needs, then hunger will not be a problem, and it will not be necessary to use appetite suppressants. This will be a choice of qualitative eating instead of quantitative. At a buffet style dinner, a double serving of vegetables with low calorie dressing will serve as filler that displaces the hunger for heavy calorie foods. Keeping away from the spare part department, such as the refrigerator and the cookie jar, will facilitate fate loss.

When one loses fat, it does not entail a loss of cells but rather a loss of cell contents because nature does not provide a vacuum. This loss enhances an urge to fill the space resulting from it. This means rapid weight loss is likely to be followed by rapid weight gain. The aroma from a well-cooked meal would sometimes appear to be filling. This is the basic reason why crash diets lead to rapid weight loss but simultaneously are followed by rapid weight gain. Hungry cells are generally flabby, and the body looks skinny or meager. The urge to regain an acceptable profile will tempt one to see this as an emancipation from a diet program that deprives one from all the good things of life. A planned diet program should be a permanent behavioral lifestyle change.

A regular exercise program strengthens cell walls and will dissipate the look of being meager or skinny. If one is unable to join a gym, then daily walks will do just as well. Proper dieting and consistent exercise will not only enhance good health but will build a strong immunity against prevailing viruses and contagious diseases.

For more detailed information visit *http://1ref.us/81*

Surviving Stress

Although it is not a disease, stress, which is an everyday fact of life, can be as debilitating as a disease. Stress is unavoidable, so we must learn how to appropriately deal with it. Stress involves changes ranging from the negative extreme of actual physical danger to the excitement of falling in love or breaking up a love affair. Not all stress is bad. Stress sometimes is desirable. Good or bad, it is how one responds to life's changing experiences that determines the impact stress will have on one's life.

Following are practical recommendations for surviving stress and turning the negative into positive:

- Don't read your incoming correspondence or bills at night. It might be a bad way to end a day.
- Don't premeditate tomorrow's problems.
- Live one day at a time.
- Don't try to solve the impossible.
- Don't worry about what you wish you had.
- Don't worry about what you think others might say.
- Don't worry about what might or could have happened.
- Don't worry about what you should have done and did not do.
- Don't worry about past mistakes or failures.
- Don't worry about disappointments.
- If what you had broke, mend it or forget it.
- If the way seems dark, don't panic or give up; keep heart. The darkest part of night is the moment just before daylight. Keep looking up; there is hope ahead.
- If you are down, your next move is up.
- If you have suffered a loss, you are going to appreciate gain. So forget your losses and start preparing for your gain.
- It takes more energy to frown than to smile. So conserve your energy. Start smiling and keep on doing it.
- Stop complaining because it triggers stress. Give thanks for whatever you have. It could be ten times worse. There are many who are worse off.
- The best remedy for stress is exercise.
- Think, live, and act positively. Every night is followed by a day, and there is always calm after every storm.
- If going west makes you unhappy, then turn around and go east. Change can sometimes relax the mind.

Biographical Sketch

Born on October 5, 1930, Robert Elkanah Williams is the last of eleven children. He was born and raised in a country village known as Saint Toolis in the parish of Manchester, Jamaica, West Indies. This village is four miles from the nearest town, two miles from the post office and one mile from the primary school. He walked every Friday to the town to shop, every Wednesday to the post office to collect the mail, and every day to school. There were days when he had to go home for lunch during the noon hour and make it back to school within one hour.

Robert knew little to nothing about his father. He grew up with his mother who was a dressmaker and a dedicated mother. By the time he reached third grade, he became a loner because all his other siblings had finished school. There were no high schools except the Jamaica Government Local Examinations, which, when taken successfully, were considered equivalent to a high school certificate. Thus at age fifteen, 90 percent of students finished their educational career and did not see it necessary to study for the first, second and third year local examinations.

His family kept goats for milk, chickens for eggs, and a garden for vegetables and food. They had a lot of citrus fruit trees such as oranges, tangerines, and grapefruits, as well as avocados, breadfruit, and coffee. His mother was somewhat independent and thus was highly respected by the community as a whole.

Robert still remembers getting up at 6:00 a.m. every day to tend to the goats, feed the chickens, and do something in the garden. By 8:00 a.m. he was on his way to school. At noon he ran home for lunch and had to be back at school by 1:00 p.m. If he was five minutes late, his teacher would whip him. He finished primary school by the time he was thirteen years old because he was promoted, which eliminated some of the forms. During the remaining two years of his required schooling, he studied for the Jamaica local examinations and passed them.

In 1946 Robert worked in a book and bible store in Kingston, and the following year saw him knocking on the doors of businesses in search of a job. His search was futile, and he went back to live with his mother in Saint Toolis. At home his neighbors tried, without success, to have his mother protect him from evil spirits by wearing some type of guard prescribed by a witch doctor.

In 1950 with the help of his brother Robert entered West Indian Training College. After three years he graduated from the ministerial course. College days were very challenging. Since he had finished school in 1946, he was only qualified to be in Form IV, but after persistent appeal, he was granted the privilege of sitting for the Senior Cambridge Overseas Examination. This was a real challenge as his classmates had been preparing for this exam for two years. Geometry, Algebra, and Spanish were all new to Robert, but he believed in himself, and he became the first student to take the course in one year. He passed the exam with distinction. With this success, he finished a five-year course in three. He worked his way through college, graduated in 1953, and had his first job assignment as a church school principal in Petersfield Westmoreland.

In 1954 Robert married Gloria E. Rochester, the daughter of Mr. and Mrs. Claston Rochester of Bull Savannah, St. Elizabeth, Jamaica. He was transferred to Harrison Memorial High School in 1955 as a history and Bible teacher. During that year he held his first evangelistic crusade and baptized forty-six souls. In 1956 he was given his first pastoral district of six churches. He was ordained in 1957. By 1960 he was a senior pastor with seventeen churches and three church schools. He started up a new church known as Gibraltar and won more than 1,000 souls to Christ. By then his wife had given him four children: three boys, Bryan, Robert, and, David, and one daughter, Dollis.

In 1963 the family immigrated to the United States in answer to a call from the Southwest Regional Conference to pastor four churches: Tyler, Nacogdoches, Longview, and Marshall, Texas. In 1965 a fourth son, Noel, was born to Robert and Gloria. Two years later they were transferred to Little Rock, Arkansas, to pastor in Little Rock, Pine Bluff, Hot Springs, and Marianna. He started one church in Monroe.

In 1967 Robert began premedical studies at the University of Arkansas. After receiving his bachelor of science degree, he entered the medical school of Guadalajara, Mexico. During the next four years he sold books during the summers and preached in almost every Baptist church where he canvassed in Memphis, Tennessee; Oakland and San Francisco, California; and Lufkin, Texas. He made enough money to pay his school fees and to maintain his family. His wife stood by him all the way. When funds were low, she went back to the United States and worked. Had it not been for her, he would not have made it.

He finished medical school in 1973 and did his internship in family medicine at Cornwall Regional Hospital and in obstetrics and gynecology at Crawford Long Hospital in Atlanta, Georgia. He also completed one year of pediatrics work in Colima, Mexico, in 1975.

In 1981 his sons Bryan and David graduated from medical school. Robert graduated from dental school in 1983, and in 1986, Dollis graduated from Georgia State University with her degree in the science fields of biology and chemistry. In 1984 Noel, was at the beginning of his college career when he met in a fatal car accident.

From 1979 to 1988 Robert worked in forensic medicine under a contract with the Commonwealth of the Bahamas. In 1989 he served as the nonsmoking specialist for Georgia and later as the epidemiologist for minority health. During these years he earned his master's degree in public health (MPH) and his doctorate in holistic medicine from the University of La Salle, Louisiana.

In 1996 Robert entered into a contract with the Jamaican Ministry of Health to serve as the medical officer of health for the parish of Westmoreland. During this time he implemented a program that successfully stemmed the typhoid and dengue epidemics.

His mission has always been to serve where the need is greatest, and this he has accomplished because in each area where he served, he had the challenge of accomplishing what others saw as impossibilities. He has always served with the mentality that it is better to give than to get. He has survived a life full of adversity.

We invite you to view the complete
selection of titles we publish at:

www.TEACHServices.com

scan with your mobile
device to go directly
to our website

Please write or email us your praises, reactions, or
thoughts about this or any other book we publish at:

P.O. Box 954
Ringgold, GA 30736

Info@TEACHServices.com

TEACH Services, Inc., titles may be purchased in bulk for
educational, business, fund-raising, or sales promotional use.
For information, please e-mail:

BulkSales@TEACHServices.com

Finally if you are interested in seeing
your own book in print, please contact us at

publishing@TEACHServices.com

We would be happy to review your manuscript for free.

www.ingramcontent.com/pod-product-compliance
Lightning Source LLC
Chambersburg PA
CBHW081924170426
43200CB00014B/2827